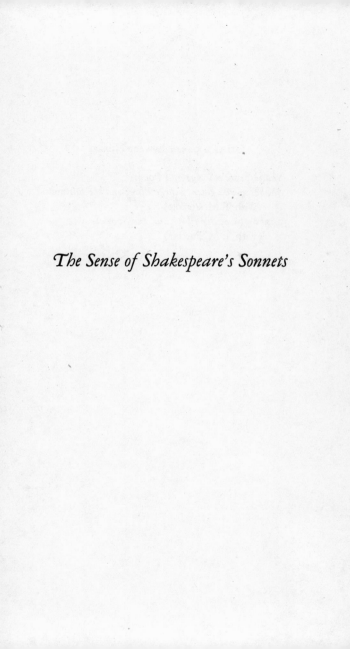

The Sense of Shakespeare's Sonnets

OTHER BOOKS BY EDWARD HUBLER

Shakespeare's Songs and Poems
Shakespeare: Twenty-three Plays and the Sonnets
    (with T. M. Parrott)
Shakespeare: Six Plays and the Sonnets
    (with T. M. Parrott)

The Sense of Shakespeare's Sonnets

BY

EDWARD HUBLER

A Dramabook

 HILL AND WANG
NEW YORK

First Dramabook Edition January 1962

Manufactured in the United States of America

567890

TO ELIZABETH HARRY

Acknowledgments

D URING the years in which I have been turning this little book over in my mind I have amassed an indebtedness which I can only begin to acknowledge. Specific acknowledgments are recorded in the notes, but there are other debts, larger and more pervasive: to my professors, and now my friends, Thomas Marc Parrott and Charles Grosvenor Osgood, who long ago encouraged my interest in the poetry of the Renaissance; to Professor Willson Coates of the University of Rochester, Professor Walter B. Scott of Northwestern University, and Professor Homer Woodbridge of Wesleyan University, who read and corrected the next to the last version of the manuscript of this book; to the erudition of Professor Alba Warren, now an officer of the Army of the United States, to Professor William Ringler of Washington University, to Professor Robert Hallwachs and Mr. Robert Towers of Princeton University, to Professor Alfred Harbage of Columbia University, and to Mr. Christian Paul Gruber of Grinnell College.

There are still other debts: to the English Institute for permission to use material which appeared in *English Institute Essays, 1948*; to my university for a term free from teaching duties; to the books one absorbs and never quotes from, the invaluable *Les Sonnets Élizabéthains*, for example, by Janet Scott; to the books one reads and dislikes and learns from because he cannot bear to leave their arguments as he found them; to volumes like the New Variorum edition of the sonnets which one uses constantly and takes for granted; to conversations with the late Harley Granville-Barker; to the late Professor Asher Hinds, who finished a day in the classroom only to begin teaching his confreres; and to the questions of students and the encouragement of friends.

June 1951   EDWARD HUBLER

Edward Hubler is Professor of English at Princeton University where he has taught for more than twenty-five years.

Contents

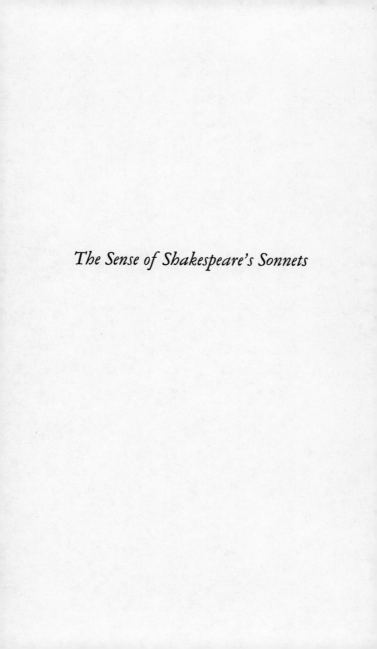

The Sense of Shakespeare's Sonnets

Introduction

WITH the possible exception of *Hamlet*, none of Shakespeare's works has been the object of more investigation nor the subject of more controversy than the little book of sonnets published in 1609. The reader may well suppose that everything worth saying about them has been said—and perhaps it has. They have been subjected to endless scrutiny in the search for further biographical knowledge of Shakespeare and in the attempts to identify the unnamed persons addressed in them. There has been a continued effort ever since their second printing in 1640 to arrange them in a more satisfactory order than that of the first edition, usually with a view to making them tell a more coherent story. In our time there has been a prolonged and fruitful consideration of their relation to the conventions of the sonnet tradition. Yet there has been little critical attention paid to them as poems, and except for the attempt to establish the date of their composition by comparing their stylistic qualities with those of the plays, they have not been considered in relation to the rest of Shakespeare's work. Their content has, in our time, been found to be of little interest. The truth is that apart from studies in the history of ideas, thought has been at a discount in modern criticism, and in Shakespeare criticism the dominant fashion, now a half century old, asserts in all solemnity that Shakespeare "had no mind" or that "if he thought he thought to no purpose." It is a point of view peculiar to our age. Coleridge, whose best remarks on Shakespeare are still the best there are, called him the "myriad-minded Shakespeare." If we persuade ourselves that Shakespeare thought to no purpose, it can only be because we will not recognize that the creation of enduring poems and plays is conceivably purpose enough for a poet and playwright, or that the thought is not our thought. But if we assume, at least as a kind of working hypothesis, that Shakespeare's mind was probably as good as our own, it might not be useless to consider for a while even some of his most commonplace ideas, such as those which the sonnets disclose.

It is obvious that the young Shakespeare was able to express his most characteristic ideas and attitudes in poems before he was able to objectify them in the more troublesome medium of the drama, for it was in poetry that he first achieved distinction, that he first acquired the craftsmanship to take, in Yeats' phrase, "the first plunge away from himself." He was a poet and a capital teller of stories before he was a dramatist of comparable stature. His first comedy was a brilliant elaboration of one of Plautus' plots, unequaled at that time in English drama for its narrative skill; but you may read it through without finding a suggestion of what Shakespeare was later to be, or, if you do, it will only be that, knowing the full-blown plant, you can recognize its seed. The play has a sweetness unknown to Plautus, the absence of which is Plautus' strength, but there is nothing of the strength that we can describe only as Shakespearean. There is nothing that pierces and little that sings; it is pure story. From the beginning Shakespeare, who was Marlowe's exact contemporary, could tell a story as Marlowe never learned to tell one (Marlowe's best told story is unfinished); but had he died with Marlowe, there would be little besides some early sonnets to indicate the superiority of his genius.

Of the early work that is wholly Shakespeare's *The Comedy of Errors* is farce, *Titus Andronicus* melodrama. Each is a story of action; each is as pure an instance of its kind as anything he was ever to write, and not because of a respect for genres, but because that is what he could do. With *Two Gentlemen of Verona* he moves toward comedy, with *Richard III* toward tragedy, and the progress is marked by what he is able to give these stories over and above physical action. *Venus and Adonis* is a conscious bid for literary reputation, and *The Rape of Lucrece*, in his own words a "graver labour," is a conscious moving toward the meaningfulness by which the horror of melodrama rises to the realm of tragedy. There is no clearer index of Shakespeare's rise in stature as a dramatist than his increasing power to incorporate in his stories what Melville called the "flashings-forth of the intuitive truth in him, those short quick probings at the very axis of reality." The flashings and probings found their first considerable expression in the sonnets, in Shakespeare's lyric expression of his perceptions of friendship, of love and lust, of growth through experience, of sin and expiation, of his notions of mutability, plenitude, and reputation, of poetry and the craft of the writer. These are the ideas with which this study is concerned.

I should like to approach these matters with as little tedium as possible, without a defense of all my assumptions. Later at appropriate points I shall do what I can to justify them. However, there are one or two questions which had better be considered now. I have assumed an early date for the sonnets. In the total absence of external evidence which would fix a precise date, it seems proper to accept the internal evidence which places them early in Shakespeare's career. I believe that they were written over a period of four or five years beginning in 1592. This conclusion is conservative enough and accords with the opinion of reputable scholars with no axes to grind. I have assumed a certain rough order for the sonnets. It seems that the precise order of their composition cannot be established on the basis of our present knowledge; certainly it has not been established up to now. Still, if one is to read the sonnets at all, they must be read in some sequence, and the traditional order, that of the first edition, is highly imperfect, as everybody knows, having no greater authority than that of the publisher of the sonnets, who had them printed without Shakespeare's consent and without the benefit of the author's supervision. I believe that the soundest approach to a reordering of the sonnets is that of the late Tucker Brooke, on whose work I shall sometimes depend. However, an exact reordering of the sonnets is not essential to our purpose.

As originally printed, the sonnets fall into three groups: numbers 1-126, which are addressed to, or are concerned with, a young man; numbers 127-152, addressed to or concerned with a young lady; and numbers 153-154, free translations of a Greek poem, made presumably to be given to a lady who was going to Bath and having no connection with the other sonnets. There is no reason to suppose that any sonnet in either of the first two groups belongs in the other. The English language being what it is, references to gender are sometimes ambiguous; but when the references are clear, those in the first group refer to a man and those in the second to a woman. There are no exceptions. It is apparent from what they tell us that the first two groups were written concurrently. But what do they tell us?

They tell of four people: Shakespeare, who speaks in the first person, another poet, a young man, and a young woman. In the original edition and all sensible rearrangements, the sonnets open with a series of poems praising the young man's beauty and urging him to beget a child. He is young, handsome, of good family, of gentle disposition, and, it appears, the possessor of boundless virtues. He is told that youth and beauty are brief, that fatherhood is a duty to himself and to the world, and that his qualities must be preserved in the immortality which children can bestow. Toward the end of the opening sequence Shakespeare promises the young man another immortality—he will eternize him in poems that will never die.

After a while other poets began to address verses to the young man. One of them, a poet of greater power than the rest, Shakespeare regards as a rival, fearing that he will come between the young man and him, for as the sonnets proceed, the friendship takes on a symbolic value for Shakespeare, becoming the emblem of hope in a changing and discouraging world of unrealized desires. In the meantime Shakespeare has acquired a mistress, a woman younger than he, attractive with an unfashionable beauty, and quite without principles. For a time he is contented in their love, but it soon appears that he does not rest easily in the complications of a double infidelity, for she too is married; and when her aggressive unfaithfulness extends to the seduction of the young man, Shakespeare finds himself in a situation growing more and more unbearable. Forced to break the triangle, he chooses the friend and rejects the lady.

It is sometimes said that Shakespeare's preference for the young man indicates a homosexual relation between them. A reasonable consideration of this matter cannot be brief, and, since it has no bearing on the main part of this study, it has been reserved for the appendix. It is more often said that the sonnets represent the idealization of masculine friendship over the love of man for woman, but this is at best a partial truth. The question involves a concept of love. Throughout his works Shakespeare distinguishes between love and lust, and his distinction is that of the ordinary man. When to the sexual basis of the love of man and woman there is added, at the very least, a mutual liking and mutual interests, Shakespeare is content to call it love. The attraction to the young woman is presented in the sonnets as purely sexual and does not begin to exhaust the concept of love appearing in Shakespeare's works as a whole. It would be more truthful to say that in the sonnets Shakespeare chooses a significant masculine friendship over an uncomfortable and illicit sexual entanglement, but that is so sensible a preference that it has not been generally observed, even after all these years and all the pains that Shakespeare has taken to set it forth. The truth is that the general reader seldom reads the sonnets through, and the scholar who reads them through sometimes does so halfheartedly, as a scholarly duty or to document some previously formed notion. And so the old ideas about them persist. There is some motivation to this. The excellence of the sonnets *is* an excellence of parts. Most of the sonnets are not first-rate poems, and many of them are obscure. The sequence, it appears, was not designed with a view to creating an overall effect, and is wretchedly frustrating for the reader who innocently supposes that a sequence of poems by Shakespeare will naturally tell a story.

The sonnets are not narrative poems. They are a collection of lyrics on a variety of subjects expressing a variety of moods and psychological states. Now and then they fall into a sequence, or can be placed in one, but quite without the order one expects from a storyteller of Shakespeare's skill. In the sonnet sequences of the Renaissance, both in England and on the continent, there is little story element. To be sure there is more in Shakespeare's sonnets than in some others, and there is more in Spenser's and Sidney's than in his; but in none is the story primary. One uses the word "story" only because there is no other word for it. What story there is in Shakespeare's sequence is implied, and, although it extends over several years, is almost barren of events—a curiously uncharacteristic state of affairs in Shakespearean narrative. If Shakespeare had set out to tell a story he surely would have told it better. It may be that the sonnets were written as verse letters, and one of them, in fact, says very plainly that it is a sort of letter. All things considered, there is much to support the view which holds that the sonnets are a series of verse letters written to two people on the subject of the poet's relation to them. The difficulty here is that once we think of the sonnets as letters we tend to ascribe a literalness to them which it would be dangerous to take for granted, for whatever the sonnets *may* be, they *are* poems, and a poem is not necessarily the precise record of an actual happening. We should remember what Da Vinci long ago remarked, that art has two subjects, man and man's hopes. The glimpses we get of Shakespeare and his friends in the sonnets may either show them as they were or as, at the moment, he wanted them to be. But whether the sonnets were or were not letters, or whether the reflections of persons in them are or are not historically accurate, is not a matter of primary concern with us. If one takes poetry to be a manifestation of recollected emotion, it is possible to argue that in the sonnets Shakespeare "unlocked his heart"; but if we assume that through the recollection and in the act of composition the poet's emotion might have been transmuted into something which had not existed before, we cannot so readily take the step from poetry to biography. We are here concerned with *what the sonnets say*. Whether they are or are not historically accurate is a question beyond the range of this study.

There are many reasons for the obscurity of the sonnets. Sometimes they refer to events of which there is no knowledge, and until the events are known, the obscurities arising from these references must stand. Sometimes the sonnets are obscure because Shakespeare did not take the trouble to write well, or because he allowed himself to be overingenious. But chiefly the sonnets puzzle by the way they glance at ideas without a specific statement of them, by their assumption of a knowledge of the way the poet's mind worked. It is with this last sort of obscurity, together with the natural complexity of Shakespeare's mind, that this study will be concerned.

If we have learned anything from the mode of criticism dominant in our time, we ought to have an approach as useful for the sonnets as for modern poems. If we were uncertain of the force of an image in, say, Yeats, we would go through his poems in search of other uses of the image in an attempt to discover the notions he habitually associated with it. It has lately been a custom of Shakespeare criticism, when troubled by the obscurity of Shakespeare's meanings, to go through the works of other Renaissance poets in order to discover what a statistical abstraction known as "the Elizabethans" thought of the matter. It is assumed that this will tell us what Shakespeare meant, and in so far as it does, the method is all to the good; but it is not enough, for it ignores the poet's individuality. The most patent thing about Shakespeare is that although he was a man of his time, he was not precisely like his contemporaries. If he had been, who but an antiquarian would care about him? Perhaps some of his thought will be more clearly understood if we examine it against the background of his time *and* the poetic personality which his works reveal.

Form and Matter

THE notion of Shakespeare as the natural poet, the artist of direct self-expression, is now an old one. It has survived many literary fashions and many revolutions in thinking about nature. To the young Milton, Shakespeare was "fancy's child" and his poetic effects were both "wild" and "native." At about the time that Milton was referring to Shakespeare in this way, John Benson found the sonnets, in his 1640 edition of them, "serene, cleere, and eligantly plaine"; and ever since then there have been critics to praise them for their naturalness and simplicity, although they are, in all truth, difficult enough. If the matter is considered relatively—the sonnets in relation to other contemporary sonnets, and the verses in general in relation to, say, Milton's—there is some justification for the opinion. Some of the sonnets are simple, and sometimes Shakespeare's dramatic writing is simpler than that of any other poet who has achieved comparable effects. No other English dramatist in a similar context has dared to be as simple as he is in the "Good-night, sweet prince" speech toward the close of *Hamlet*. He had learned to write, and, in Miss Stein's phrase, it had become a "natural thing to do. But there are others who learn how, they learn to read and write, but they read and write as if they knew how."[1] It is well said. Although he had a talent for the natural and simple, the power of simple expression was not his from the beginning; it grew with his art and is only one aspect of it, but the one which, how often and how wrongly! is taken for the whole. In the commonly held view simplicity equals sincerity, and, conversely, complexity is artificial. The praiseworthy thing is the simple thing. "An artist," writes Hesketh Pearson in a

[1] Gertrude Stein, *Four in America*, Yale University Press, New Haven, 1947, p. 120.

discussion of the sonnets, "does not fool about with words when expressing his true emotion."[2] Pearson's study of Shakespeare is a deservedly popular book, popular enough to have been distributed to the armed forces during the Second World War.

The view of the sonnets which has dominated learned criticism for the past fifty years is at first glance a different matter. It was given currency by the late Sir Sidney Lee, who, toward the end of the last century, was engaged in demonstrating Shakespeare's indebtedness to his predecessors and contemporaries. Lee, having pointed out with notable clarity and learning the existence of certain sonnet conventions, concluded that the sonnets were conventional and little more, for he tended, like Pearson, to value only the spontaneous. In one of his sonnets Shakespeare had written,

> When I have seen the hungry ocean gain
> Advantage on the kingdom of the shore,

and Lee, noticing that Shakespeare had come across the idea in Golding, supposed that Shakespeare's statement was without meaning.[3] We need not look into the logic of this; still less should we wonder if Shakespeare really had seen the phenomenon. The point is that for Sir Sidney repetition constituted convention, convention was empty, and the sonnets therefore appeared to be insincere. In this view of poetry a poem's value is finally determined by reference to documents other than the poem itself, and this is very much like Pearson's second measure of value. He tells us that we can recognize the sincerity of certain passages in Shakespeare by, first, their simplicity, and, second, "because they tell us what we already knew about him."[4] In both the learned and the

[2] Hesketh Pearson, *A Life of Shakespeare*, Penguin Books, 1942, p. 27.

[3] Sir Sidney Lee, *A Life of William Shakespeare*, The Macmillan Company, New York, 1931 (14th ed.), p. 32.

[4] *op.cit.*, p. 30.

popular view there is, then, a limitation on the function of poetry which Shakespeare was not willing to admit. A reading of the sonnets makes it quite clear that Shakespeare believed, or wanted the reader to believe, that they were a true expression of his <u>individuality</u>. "Every word doth almost tell my name," he wrote in one of them, "Showing their birth and where they did proceed." Shakespeare has a good many remarks on his particular purpose in writing the sonnets, and on poetic theory in general, and I think that the student should not reject them without due consideration. I hope that it will not be idle to consider them in relation to Shakespeare's poetic practice.

The most cursory reading of Shakespeare will make it clear that he liked to play with words, sometimes with wretched effect; and it ought to be equally plain that no man without an interest in words and word patterns ever became a poet. Shakespeare's native interest in words was encouraged by the tradition of his time which considered the art of writing to be based on a body of precepts and saw no reason to think of craftsmanship as an affectation. Craftsmanship was then known to be what it is—the means by which the thing is said. Now it happens that it is in the nature of conscious artists to be seduced at times into an overemphasis of their craft, and this matters very little to an age which takes an interest in technique. In such times there is an allowance, and quite without condescension, for the performer's pride in skill. The composers of concertos used to allow the performer to provide his own cadenza, to do, in effect, what he could, and simply in order to show what he could do. There was a tendency in Shakespeare's time, and earlier, to admire the formal dexterity of ingenious word play, and this is nowhere better illustrated than in the sonnet tradition. Petrarch, whose exquisite taste saved him from the greatest excesses, was a master at it. One of his sonnets is an elaboration of an image comparing his lady to the sun. She is the

sun; her person, her face, her eyes, her hair are suns. If the
sun rises before her, he shines brightly; but when she arises,
he is dimmed. Petrarch loved to play upon the similarity
of his lady's name (Laura) to *l'aura* (the breeze) and *laurea*
(the laurel) and to resolve words similar to her name
(*laureta*, for example) into its syllables and expand them in
terms of praise. All this can be boring enough in Petrarch;
in his imitators it often becomes a dreary elaboration of
empty virtuosity.

Shakespeare, too, sometimes let his virtuosity get the better
of him, as certain spectacular failures in the sonnets to the
young man testify:

> To me, fair friend, you never can be old,
> For as you were when first your eye I ey'd. . . .[5]

The modern reader wonders how Shakespeare brought himself to do it. Such passages occur too often to be oversights,
and what we know of Shakespeare's poetic practice does not
allow us to think that he disliked them. The banished Romeo
grieves that he must go to Mantua while every other person
and every thing may stay in Verona with Juliet: "This flies
may do, but I from this must fly." Considered simply as
form, the line is superb—ten monosyllables arranged almost
in their prose order, yet managing to involve two antitheses:
the pun and the double use of "this." Shakespeare places "but
I" in the middle of the line, leaving on either side phrases
of exactly the same duration. The words, as it is customary
to remark of the lights in Times Square, would be beautiful
if only we did not know what they meant. It should be remembered that such passages are most frequent and most
flagrant in the poetry written when Shakespeare was learning his craft and taking pride in what he learned. It should
be observed, too, that it is his admiration of the phrase, and

[5] Sonnet 104.

not his concern for the metrical form, the scene, or the genre, which sometimes dominates his judgment.

Shakespeare's weakness, since it was of his age, passed almost unnoticed. There was, of course, some adverse criticism. The players, speaking of the ease with which Shakespeare composed, had said that he scarce blotted a line. "Would he had blotted a thousand," was Ben Jonson's response. This seems to be fair enough, but when Jonson proceeds to specific comment we notice that his criticism is not directed at Shakespeare's weakness. He objects to Shakespeare's making Caesar say that he "never did wrong, but with just cause." Although this is a better and wiser line than the one Shakespeare later substituted for it, Jonson nevertheless finds it ridiculous—not formally, mind you, but as an idea. Jonson's objection seems to assume that there is always a right way and that a just action never involves injustice. It is an extraordinary assumption for a man of Jonson's intellect, but, in a way, it is characteristic of him. It indicates his comparative singleness of vision, which, in turn, does much to account for the greater virulence of his comedy and his inability to conceive a living tragedy. Jonson's thought is often clearer than Shakespeare's, his poetry less textured—and precisely because of the greater simplicity of what he had to express. With him there was not the same danger of loss in pruning a phrase. He was not much interested in tangential and associated meanings. To Shakespeare, intensely aware of the many-sidedness of meaning, the play on words was a ready instrument.

In our time we seem to have agreed that the pun is worth less. It is now good form to greet a pun with groans, and not even the punster is offended. There seems to be an assumption that the pun, resulting from the accidental resemblances of words, can have nothing essential about it and is incapable of expressing value. Yet the pun persists in spite of our conviction of its frivolity. Punsters apologize, but they go on punning; and a man is allowed to pun if he deprecates the enjoyment. In Shakespeare's time the pun was a rhetorical figure, and the rhetoricians considered it solemnly, dividing it into four categories and dignifying each with a long name. In those days word play was not necessarily frivolous, and our loss of the point of view which lent puns dignity is not clear gain. A poet is made as well as born, and in the sixteenth century the making was a conscious process. The fledgling poet learned what could be done with words by studying the figures of speech. The man of our time tends to notice only the figures which do not succeed, which are not figures of thought as well as figures of speech. He cries out against the excesses and fails to notice the others, the near relations. Would he call the use of *bier* and *beard* in the following passage a pun?

> When lofty trees I see barren of leaves
> Which erst from heat did canopy the herd,
> And summer's green all girded up in sheaves,
> Born on the bier with white and bristly beard. . . .[6]

If it is a pun, do we wish it otherwise? And why not? And what are we to think of the schematic placing of *unfair* and *fairly* in the fourth line following?

> Those hours that with gentle work did frame
> The lovely gaze where every eye doth dwell,
> Will play the tyrants to the very same,
> And that unfair which fairly doth excell. . . .[7]

The line can be paraphrased, "and make unbeautiful that which now excels in beauty," but the paraphrase for all its clarity is prose. Is there any gain in the repetition of the syllable and the emphasis on the related and unrelated parts of the words? The truth is that Shakespeare's interest in

[6] Sonnet 12.   [7] Sonnet 5.

words produced some of his best as well as some of his worst effects.

There are two sonnets, numbers one hundred thirty-five and one hundred thirty-six, which are elaborate four-way puns on his name, Will, which, then as now, also meant *volition* and *obstinacy*. In his day it had the additional meaning of lust. The first begins,

> Whoever hath her wish, thou hast thy *Will*,
> And *Will* to boot, and *Will* in overplus. . . .

Although it would be possible to write a paraphrase giving the multiple meanings of each repetition, no one should be asked to read it. Readers attracted by the ingenuity will find, on piecing out the poems, that they are successful works of a kind no longer admired. They make sense, and their sense is appropriate to the context in which they are found; but they no longer impress. They are bravura pieces in an outmoded manner, and they do not pretend to be anything more. They are, moreover, the only such pieces Shakespeare ever wrote.

Since he was a poet, he inevitably admired formal graces; and since he was very human, he sometimes indulged his admiration; but his admiration never altered his conviction that matter should take precedence over form. He seems to have been primarily attracted to a given form by its potential utility, by its appropriateness to his purpose and talent. It was his way to take a known form and wrest it to his uses, transforming it, sometimes, into an instrument of an effectiveness its inventor could not have foreseen. Then when he had humbled it to his uses, it was his way to move on to something else. His technical practice throughout his career bears witness to this basic attitude, and his use of the sonnet form he adopted is a case in point. Although in two-thirds of his sonnets he placed the main pause after the twelfth line, it comes after the eighth line in twenty-seven of them, and is irregular in the remaining few. Sonnet number ninety-nine has fifteen lines, sonnet one hundred twenty-six has twelve, and is written in couplets. Number one hundred forty-five is in tetrameter verse, and all the rimes in sonnet twenty are double.

Shakespeare's sonnet form had been invented early in the century by Henry Howard, Earl of Surrey. Its fourteen lines were divided into three quatrains and a concluding couplet. In Shakespeare's characteristic use of it, the quatrains state a subject and the couplet sums it up, most often through the application of the subject to a specific situation. In the first quatrain of the familiar seventy-third sonnet, the poet compares himself to autumn leaves; in the second, to twilight; and in the third, to dying embers. From the gathering together of these images, and the poet's application of them to himself, there emerges the idea of approaching death. Then comes the couplet directed to the friend to whom the poem is addressed and stating the idea to be derived from the situation set forth in the quatrains.

> That time of year thou mayst in me behold
> When yellow leaves, or none, or few do hang
> Upon those boughs which shake against the cold,
> Bare, ruin'd choirs where late the sweet birds sang;
> In me thou see'st the twilight of such day
> As after sunset fadeth in the west,
> Which by and by black night doth take away,
> Death's second self, that seals up all in rest;
> In me thou see'st the glowing of such fire
> That on the ashes of his youth doth lie,
> As the death-bed whereon it must expire,
> Consum'd with that which it was nourish'd by;
>> This thou perceiv'st which makes thy love more strong
>> To love that well which thou must leave ere long.

There is a pause after each quatrain, the greatest coming

after the third. It was his customary usage. There are seven rimes: *abab cdcd efef gg*. Shakespeare might have chosen the Italian sonnet with its five rimes, arranged *abba abba* in the octave, and its variety of rime schemes (*cde cde*, for instance) in the sestet. But the fewer rimes of the Italian sonnet make it a more difficult form, and the absence of the couplet makes it less suited to the explicitness Shakespeare favored. The Italian sonnet was magnificently used by Milton (a more fastidious craftsman than Shakespeare), who returned to it throughout his long career as a poet, leaving on his death only eighteen sonnets in English. Apart from the sonnets in his plays, Shakespeare wrote one hundred and fifty-four, ranging in excellence from the best lyrics in the language to quite poor stuff. Given his talent, it was impossible for him to write a worthless poem, but sometimes in the sonnets it is a near thing. One gathers that he worked at a sonnet for a while, and, if it proved recalcitrant, wrote another, not always throwing the first one away. It is notable that the English poets distinguished for their craftsmanship have almost always preferred the Italian sonnet form.

The sonnet, of whatever form, has an affinity for intensity, and the best sonnets, of whatever time and place, are those devoted to the development of a single mood, the elaboration of a single image, or the expression of a single thought. The long line (five feet in English, six in French) is admirably suited to dignified and serious expression, and the number of lines is appropriate to the sonnet's singleness of purpose. A poem intending to be both unified and intense must be long enough to permit development and short enough to allow the reader a retention of everything his eye takes in, from the first to the last words. For this purpose fourteen lines were found to be right. A few more or less would have done, but half as many would have been too few, and half again the number would have been too many. When the sonnet form was in the process of creation, son-

nets were written in varying lengths; but the form crystallized
at fourteen lines for the reasons given. Within this form it
is necessary to make everything contribute to the proposed
effect, for the tightness throws into relief everything which
does not contribute, or does so only obliquely. The sonneteer
intent on unity must either increase the matter to fit the form
or fuse both with all the skill in his power. If he permits
himself to stretch the matter, there can be no intensity; and,
in any case, verbal expansion was not Shakespeare's way.
He had no need to pad his lines; the talent for the right
word was in his flesh like blood. Although the need for a
rime sometimes forces him into brief verbosity, he has nothing at all like "Ten times in the revolving year plus three,"
a line of our century which stretches the idea of thirteen
times a year to pentameter length. But at times he would
not trouble to develop his thematic structure to a coincidence
with the sonnet form, or to articulate the parts.

In the sonnets of characteristically Shakespearean structure,
the first aspect of the idea carries through the quatrains, leaving as the technical problem of greatest difficulty the articulation of the couplet. The proportion of failures in meeting
this problem is smaller in those sonnets in which the main
pause comes after the eighth line, or thereabouts, leaving in
the remainder of the poem (equivalent to the sestet in the
Italian sonnet) enough scope to avoid the oversententious
and sometimes casual tone into which the brevity of the
couplet sometimes trapped him. One of these sonnets, number thirty-five, is a case in point. It is one of Shakespeare's
lesser poems, yet in his treatment of the couplet he achieves
a greater coherence than is usual with sonnets of like calibre
written in his accustomed form. His success with modestly
ambitious poems in which the main pause comes after the
eighth line is not without exception, but it is normal enough
to be worth notice. His technical practice in the sonnets is
of a piece with that of his plays. It is sometimes perfect,

often brilliant, too often impatient and content to let well enough alone.

In the sonnets he states his admiration for the craftsmanship of the rival poet, but the importance he accords to it does not permit him to admire the poems, for he always grants priority to substance. There is nothing in his works indicating anything but dislike for the "fools . . . that for a tricksy word defy the matter."[8] He praises plain speaking and sends satiric shafts at the spinners of "taffeta phrases, silken terms precise" that blow one "full of maggot ostentation."[9] The attitude is everywhere expressed—in the young courtier who so outraged Hotspur, and in Osric, whom Hamlet found not worth his scorn. Shakespeare was a professional writer, but he was not a man of letters; his love of literature did not lead him to tolerate the "literary." He never accepted the idea of style as an end in itself. We are sometimes told that his plays disclose a low view of the writing profession, but I think it is rather that his comic genius kept him aware of the eccentricities of his craft. Hotspur's contempt for "mincing poetry" discloses the common attitude of the man of affairs; it also discloses Shakespeare's awareness of the too frequent justification of it. Some poetry *is* mincing, and some writers are fools, as Shakespeare well knew. From time to time he falls into the "literary," but these descents are failures of taste and, usually, of youth. His conviction was always against the subordination of the thought to the word.

In the sonnets addressed to the young man he contrasts his own expressions of devotion with the "strained touches rhetoric can lend"[10] to the works of other poets, assuring the reader that the old strain needs no variation and declining to employ the latest literary mannerisms.[11] He tells the reader

---

[8] *The Merchant of Venice*, 3.5.74.
[9] *Love's Labours Lost*, 5.2.409.
[10] Sonnet 82. [11] Sonnet 76.

that he wants the sonnets to represent him as he is, and that he believes they do.[12] On another occasion he remarks that the sonnet is sent "to witness duty, not to show my wit."[13] The assurance must be taken with the realization that there is no necessary contradiction between showing both duty and wit in the same poem, for it is obvious that in poetry a condition of complete artlessness is impossible. The appearance of artlessness is another matter. And surely the normally complex reader can be moved by a poem and admire its art at the same time. There can be no question of content *or* art; there must be both; it is a matter of proportion and purpose. The truth is that quite often the sonnets do not show the craftsmanship they should, that the reader sometimes finds the lack of variation all too apparent and is too often confronted with statement that is only partially realized as poetry. The matter of some of the sonnets would be more available if they had more art.

The poet's problem was to formalize and verbalize his thought. It is, of course, only an egregious obstinacy which would refuse to suppose that sometimes it was not the other way about, that at times the phrase came first, demanding to be used. But it could not have been generally so. With him *invention*, as with the Elizabethans as a whole, had the primary meaning of finding, not the means of expression, but subject matter for composition; and the sonnets which discuss invention assure us that the subject matter (the friend and the poet's relation to him) is *given*. That is never questioned. What troubles Shakespeare is his inability to handle the subject matter. He insists on the inadequacy of "my pupil pen," a phrase which recalls the references to "my unpolished lines" and "my untutored lines" in the dedications to *Venus and Adonis* and *The Rape of Lucrece*. Although the attitude they express is opposed to Shakespeare's promises of immortality, one would have to have a very wooden no-

---

[12] Sonnet 76.　　　　　　[13] Sonnet 26.

tion of mankind to suppose them meaningless. With the greater number of persons confidence is not unwavering, especially professional confidence at the beginning of their careers, and the lives of poets for whom documentation is adequate show periodic resurgences of doubt to be a common experience. Such is the case in the sonnets, but we should notice that it is not a simple alternation of confidence and fear. The poet's sense of inadequacy is set forth in relation to particular matters: he is not equal to his theme, or he is not of the calibre of the other poet, or both. In sonnet number seventy-nine he says that the greatness of this theme deserves the "travail of a worthier pen," and in the succeeding poem he calls the rival poet a "better spirit" and refers to "my saucy bark, inferior far to his."

It is customary to say that the praise of the other poet is grudgingly given, and it is clearly far from wholehearted. Yet there are aspects of the other man's writing which won Shakespeare's admiration. What he disliked about the rival poet was the character of the man. In the eighty-sixth sonnet there is the well-known and enigmatic passage about the "affable familiar ghost" which "nightly gulls" the other poet with intelligence. We cannot know to what rumored events the phrase refers, and we may dispute the meaning of some of the words, but it is clear that Shakespeare suggests something specious about the content of the rival's poems. We gather from many references that Shakespeare considered him an opportunist who praised the young man for reasons other than those of honest friendship. To this pretension, he says, even the graces of the subject can bring only a superficial virtue; they can "but mend the style."[14] The context of the verses about the rival poet is complicated, and their force is far from single, yet the element of deference, varied in expression and stated at times with bitterness, is present,

[14] Sonnet 78.

called forth by the other poet's style—"the proud full sail of his great verse."[15] What Shakespeare praises in the other poet is technical proficiency. What he deplores in his own work is the lack of it.

Since the identity of the other poet is unknown, we cannot weigh the truth of Shakespeare's estimate of him, but it is obvious that his opinions of his own work are on the whole just. In the sonnets the lowest level of excellence is low indeed, but the subject matter of the worst verses is usually that for which in other poems he has been able to find adequate expression. Clearly the normal difficulty is not one of substance; it is the failure to mold the subject matter into a coherent poem. Sometimes he begins a sonnet in an excellent vein and ends it wretchedly. Number one hundred eleven is a case in point. Up to the couplet a poem of considerable stature, it is boundlessly interesting as a statement of a recurrent attitude toward his life in the theatre. With the couplet there is a change in tone and a shocking decrease in magnitude. The idea in the couplet is of course pertinent to what goes before, if only because an assurance of friendship is always proper to a series of poems addressed to a friend; but in this case the assurance comes with such a diminution of force that one wonders why it was allowed to stand.

> O, for my sake do you with Fortune chide,
> The guilty goddess of my harmful deeds,
> That did not better for my life provide
> Than public means which public manners breeds.
> Thence comes it that my name receives a brand,
> And almost thence my nature is subdu'd
> To what it works in, like the dyer's hand.
> Pity me, then, and wish I were renew'd;
> Whilst, like a willing patient, I will drink

[15] Sonnet 86.

Potions of eisel 'gainst my strong infection;
No bitterness that I will bitter think,
Nor double penance, to correct correction.
  Pity me then, dear friend, and I assure ye
  Even that your pity is enough to cure me.

The artistic failure of the couplet is so accentuated by the double rime that one wonders if at the time of composition the ingenuity of the rime seemed to justify the couplet.

Perhaps we can learn more of Shakespeare's poetic practice if we turn to a structural pattern with which he always succeeded. No sonnet beginning with "When" is an undistinguished poem. Naturally there is nothing magical in the word. It is simply that "when" introduces a subordinate clause which must, perhaps after more subordinate matter, lead to a main clause, thus creating an arrangement of logically ordered elements in an emphatic sequence. When the arrangement can be readily made to coincide with the sonnet length, the structure avoids Shakespeare's most characteristic faults as a sonneteer—the tacked-on couplet and the broken back. He is almost certain to succeed when the parts of the sonnet stand in a "When I, Then I, Then I, So" relationship, or in some variant of it. It was an excellent pattern for a poet impatient with technical problems. But if the pattern did not reach to the end of the sonnet, or if there was no "so" or "for" notion to follow the logical sequence, the couplet, as in the fifteenth sonnet, stood in danger of seeming to be tacked on. Too often the development of the idea ends with the quatrains, and the couplet fails to share the power in which the quatrains were conceived. In such instances the couplet is poetically, but not intellectually, false. It seems, to use Shakespeare's words, to have been begotten in "the ventricle of memory . . . and delivered upon the mellowing of occasion."

Not marble nor the gilded monuments
Of princes shall outlive this powerful rime,
But you shall shine more bright in these contents
Than unswept stone besmear'd with sluttish time.
When wasteful war shall statues overturn,
And broils root out the work of masonry,
Nor Mars his sword nor war's quick fire shall burn
The living record of your memory.
'Gainst death and all-oblivious enmity
Shall you pace forth; your praise shall still find room,
Even in the eyes of all posterity
That wear this world out to the ending doom.
    So, till the judgement that yourself arise,
    You live in this, and dwell in lovers' eyes.[16]

A deservedly famous poem, it ends in a couplet of diminished force, but not because of what the couplet *says*. The promise of immortality so pallidly stated in the couplet is expressed with vigorous conviction in the preceding lines, with which, spiritually, the poem ends. The quatrains had used up the poet's emotion, leaving no power for a repetition of only formal necessity. The couplet serves chiefly to fill out the form and betray critics who, noticing the relaxed feeling, assume hastily that the theme is alien to Shakespeare's sensibility; but this cannot possibly have been the case, for the idea had been congenial enough only a few lines earlier. In general the couplet is used most expertly when its idea follows in logical sequence from the thematic structure of what has gone before, or when its function is a clear and positive summing up or application of the preceding matter, as in the seventy-third and the one hundred and sixteenth sonnets.

Tucker Brooke observed[17] that the couplet sometimes "in-

---

[16] Sonnet 55.
[17] Tucker Brooke, *Shakespeare's Sonnets*, Oxford University Press, London-New York, 1936, p. 4.

troduces a surprise or negation which suddenly swings the
reader into a point of view antithetical to that developed in
the quatrains." It may be of some significance that of the
thirteen sonnets[18] using the couplet in this way only one,
number thirty, is among the best known, and it, perhaps,
hardly deserves the distinction that has been accorded it.
Presumably it has won its place in the public's esteem
through the beauty of its opening lines:

> When to the sessions of sweet silent thought
> I summon up remembrance of things past . . . ,

for much of what follows is overweighted with decoration.
The alliteration of "And with old woes new wail my dear
times waste" is not as drearily flamboyant as Poe's "weary
way-worn wanderer," but it is a close call. In this sonnet the
casualness of the couplet is saved from emphasis by the relaxed lines which lead up to it. But generally Shakespeare's
failures with the couplet are owing to a danger inherent in
the sonnet form which he chose and to his impatience with
formal problems.

There are other failures arising from sources quite beyond
the poet's control, just as there are graces which providence
seems to have conferred uniquely on him. Both of them
can be readily noticed in the sonnets written on the subject
of absence.[19] None of these sonnets is among Shakespeare's
most distinguished poems. Too often they seem to have been
written only to witness duty, and at their worst they are his
nearest approach to frigidity. The least interesting are those
most wholly devoted to absence, and the cause of their lack
of distinction is apparent. It was the habit of his time to
think of friendship's community of interest in terms of
identity (one soul in two bodies), a metaphorical extrava-

[18] Sonnets 19, 30, 34, 42, 60, 84, 86, 91, 92, 131, 133, 139, 141.
[19] The sonnets clearly written in absence are: 27, 28, 36, 37, 38, 39,
43, 44, 45, 46, 47, 48, 49, 50, 51, 56, 57, 58, 59, 97, 98, 113, 114.

gance for which he has been censured, but which is absurd
or meaningless only to those of a literal turn of mind, or to
those who would reserve it for the poetry of romantic love.
In Shakespeare's time it was an accepted manner of speaking about a psychological fact, as Euripides wrote about
Aphrodite without, presumably, believing in her physical
reality. For Shakespeare it was, as an ideological structure
must always be for a poet, a formalized extension of his own
perception.

In his selection of already formalized ideas, the poet always takes a chance. He cannot pick them with an eye to
posterity, for he has no means of knowing which ideas will
endure and which will not. He must write for himself and
the readers of his own generation, and for the rest he can
only hope. He must, as Day Lewis remarks,[20] "hope for the
pure luck that Donne had with the compass legs—that men
still use compasses, though they have discarded epicycles
and planispheres." For us the identity metaphor in the context of friendship has gone the way of the planisphere. And
that is not the worst of it, for it was Shakespeare's habit to
think of friendship in terms of both identity and the outmoded theory of the four elements (fire, air, earth, and
water) of which all things were thought to be made. The
belief was that physical things were made of the heavier
elements, earth and water, and things of the mind and spirit
of the other two. In Shakespeare's time references to the belief were, of course, immediately understood and spontane-
ously credited. In a pair of sonnets, numbers forty-four and
forty-five, the poet wishes that he were entirely made of the
lighter elements so that he could leap the distance to his
friend, as his thoughts and wishes, being incorporeal and
therefore free of earth and water, were able to do. One imagines that the poems were never vital, but their pretty in-

---

[20] Cecil Day Lewis, *The Poetic Image*, Oxford University Press,
New York, 1947, p. 92.

genuity must have been more telling, and their thought more forceful, when the identity metaphor was taken seriously and the content of the idea of the elements was readily available.

Only a small portion of that content is now conveyed to the average reader. The association of tears and water is plain enough to be a perpetual commonplace, and it was hardly fresh when Shakespeare used it—but it was not empty. Water being then associated with earth and opposed to fire and air, the water-tears conjunction in poetry could carry the suggestion of heaviness and earth in separation from warmth and light. This gave meaning to such passages as that in which Laertes declines to shed tears for his drowned sister: "Too much of water hast thou, poor Ophelia." At the time of its composition the line was not simply the word play it has now become; it then suggested that her body had returned, cold and lifeless, to the heavier elements. But time has taken the content of the line away, and for most of us it is an irritatingly commonplace assertion, suggesting little but crassness in the speaker and forcing the actor to hope that in the richness of the scene the line will pass unnoticed.

Sometimes conceits no longer admired in themselves are effectively employed, for the decay of an idea need not be fatal to its use in a poem, provided the force of the idea *as employed* is not single. The dramatic function of the weird sisters at the opening of *Macbeth* is immediately apparent, quite apart from the spectators' belief or disbelief in witches, because the reality of the thing for which they are the emblem is undeniable to all intelligent playgoers. In a like manner the old conceit of the conflict between the eye and the heart, or the mind and the eye, is used powerfully in the dark lady sonnets because it is there invested with the force of a moral struggle; but in the sonnets written in absence to the young man, the conceit is used ingeniously for its own sake, and time has left little but the ingenuity.

Other uses of the conceit, as in sonnet one hundred fourteen, succeed because they are endowed with a collateral intellectuality:

> Or whether doth my mind, being crown'd with you,
> Drink up this monarch's plague, this flattery?
> Or whether, shall I say, mine eye saith true. . . .

Other sonnets written in absence are interesting for what they glance at, for what they give us of the poet's mind.[21] Still others[22] derive their power from the poet's fears for the dissolution of the friendship under the blows of circumstance. These can more appropriately be considered later. The thing to notice here is the relation between the power of the poems and their subject matter. Absence was not in itself a subject which the poet could work into enduring poetry. He writes best in absence when he celebrates the friendship itself, or fears for it, or writes of absence in images which for him were always figures of thought and feeling as well as figures of speech.

He saw nature precisely and was always able to find the right words for her loveliness—"proud-pied April," for example. It is to the exercise of this talent that the absence sonnets of widest fame owe their renown. Two of them ("How like a winter" and "From you I have been absent," numbers ninety-seven and ninety-eight) are remembered for passages of unobtrusive melody and lines of easy grace:

> Nor did I wonder at the lily's white,
> Nor praise the deep vermilion in the rose. . . .

It is clearly not the summit of Shakespeare's art, but it is one of his peculiar achievements, this seemingly effortless poetry of nature: "The teeming autumn big with rich increase" and such phrases as "What old December's bareness everywhere." No other English poet has phrases of that quality,

---

[21] See Sonnets 35, 37, 38, 58, 59.   [22] See Sonnets 36, 49, 57.

and, as far as I know, none of Shakespeare's translators has been able to approximate it in other languages. Shakespeare always wrote well on nature's morning loveliness and her plenitude. Subjects for which he had an affinity, they gave these poems an excellence beyond anything that the contemplation of absence inspired in him. It is one of the most striking *données* of his poetic talent. To it even more impressive powers were shortly to be added.

With writers of stature, the development of style stands in a reciprocal relation to intellectual and spiritual growth. A writer's style can persist unchanged to the end of his career only if he remains minor. In the first years of the 1590's the young Shakespeare, mainly under the influence of Marlowe, formed a style admirably suited to his early powers. The rhythmic unit was the blank verse line, and generally the memorable phrases were those of a Marlovian rotundity, or descriptive passages of his own peculiar loveliness. One could not say of it, as Eliot said of the style of *In Memoriam*, that it was intimate with the poet's depths, for there is nothing in the first works that can properly be called depths. But he soon became conscious of the depths, and a new style had to be evolved to disclose them. By the time he was writing *Richard II*, the first style was already inadequate to the new perception, and was felt to be. He was able to characterize Richard by making him the connoisseur of surfaces and the artist in words, and by bringing him to a realization of the speciousness of appearance—in short, by endowing him with a share of his own sensibility.

Richard's most moving speeches have a greater flexibility than the best verse of the preceding plays, but their metrics are not markedly different. While Richard is less inclined to think in blank verse lengths than his predecessors, the line is still the rhythmic unit, and the run on rhythms tend to end at the caesura:

> For within the hollow crown
> That rounds the mortal temples of a king
> Keeps Death his court, and there the antic sits,
> Scoffing his state, and grinning at his pomp,
> Allowing him a breath, a little scene,
> To monarchize, be fear'd, and kill with looks,
> Infusing him with self and vain conceit,
> As if this flesh which walls about our life,
> Were brass impregnable; and humour'd thus
> Comes at the last, and with a little pin
> Bores through his castle wall, and—farewell king![23]

Or, through its propriety to the character of the hero, the poet makes effective dramatic use of his ornate style, as in the descent from the ramparts of Flint Castle, where the magnificent showmanship is both Shakespeare's and Richard's:

> Down, down I come; like glist'ring Phaeton,
> Wanting the manage of unruly jades.
> In the base court? Base court, where kings grow base,
> To come at traitors' calls and do them grace.[24]

But at other times the formalism obscures, almost obliterates, the meaning:

> Ay, no; no, ay; for I must nothing be;
> Therefore no no, for I resign to thee.[25]

Throughout the play there is little of what we are later to have in abundance, and toward the end of the play when the theatricality is over and the inwardness of Richard is the dramatist's first concern, the disparity between the ornate style and the deeply felt content, between the achieved style and the newly realized depths, is the concern of Shakespeare's deposed and imprisoned artist-hero. We discover him in

[23] *Richard II*, 3.2.160-170.
[24] *Ibid.*, 3.3.178-181.   [25] *Ibid.*, 4.1.201-202.

Pomfret Castle brooding on the difficulty of putting his misery into words:

> I have been studying how I may compare
> This prison where I live unto the world,
> And for because the world is populous,
> And here is not a creature but myself,
> I cannot do it; yet I'll hammer it out. . . . [26]

With Shakespeare himself it was never hammered out in these terms. His most deeply revealing passages are never in a style which is at once in contrast to and congruent with the depths disclosed. That is the glory of Racine, who in that respect is unchallenged. Shakespeare found a more direct solution.

There is little to suggest the solution in his first works, where in general he searched for depths with Marlovian means, or with his own adaptation of the styles of Marlowe and Spenser. But when the profundity came, when, as in the later tragedies, it was at its greatest, it was sometimes expressed in a style having at once homeliness and splendor, as in Macbeth's "I have supp'd full with horrors. . . ." In his early works he tended to reserve homeliness for prose, a practice he quickly outgrew; indeed, he departed so completely from it that by the time he wrote *King Lear* the rhythmic distinction between prose and verse had disappeared, and the movement from prose to verse is, in the greatest passages, not always to be distinguished by the ear; and when it can be, it is a difference without a distinction in kind. In *King Lear* the unpatterned rhythm of the prose is the pulsing of its spirit, and the verse, if one has got it by heart, cannot be written down again in Shakespeare's lines without consulting the text. The reader is invited to try.

The seeds of this were in Shakespeare from the beginning, and as he learned to write the shoots began to appear. Their

[26] *Ibid.*, 5.5.1-5.

growth, in the way of such developments, was not constant.
Sometimes purposely, sometimes without apparent awareness, he doubled back upon himself; but there was no stop-
ping the fitful progression. In *Romeo and Juliet* there is early
formalism and ornateness, there is fustian, there is sheer aria,
and there are promises of things to come: Romeo, dreaming
of his love, is greeted by his servant with the news of her
death:

> Her body sleeps in Capel's monument,
> And her immortal part with angels lives.

Romeo replies in a speech of startling contrast to the lyric
regularity of the servant's lines:

> Well Juliet, I will lie with thee to-night.

The accents have varied values, the rhythm is irregular, the
line is just a little in excess of pentameter length. Homely
words in their prose order making poetry as revealing of
character as any dozen lines in the play! Yet they are not
altogether simple, and in as far as they are simple, it is the
simplicity of the master of language. The increasing fre-
quency with which such passages appear is the most striking
index of Shakespeare's ability to make his art the servant
of his insights. It is, in Granville-Barker's phrase, "the power
to show us reality behind appearance, or as Shelley said, to
lift the veil from the hidden beauty—and, he could have
added, the unrecognized horror—of the world." The power
is more often demonstrated in the sonnets than in the plays
contemporary with them, because, one supposes, of the
greater difficulty of expressing perceptions in dramatic form.
In any case his most considerable power flowered first in the
poems.

What the reader remembers most vividly from the early
Venus and Adonis are vignettes of nature—bits of natural
description, and, above all, Poor Wat, the hare. What stays

ineradicably in his mind from the early sonnets is the joy in plenitude, the sadness of mutability, beauty of phrase and beauty of nature, and the virtuosity of such rhythms as,

> Sap check'd with frost, and lusty leaves quite gone,
> Beauty o'er-snow'd, and bareness everywhere.

And while the reader will continue to find these things to the end of the sonnets, it is not long until he also finds: "then hate me when thou wilt," "give not a windy night a rainy morrow," "my love is as a fever," and,

> For I have sworn thee fair and thought thee bright,
> Who art as black as hell, as dark as night.

Examples swarm to be quoted, and in an instant pass from the depiction of homeliness to the unveiling of horror. In this unveiling Shakespeare sometimes displayed the old extravagance of his earlier ornateness. In an almost Strindbergian poem[27] on the power of lust, he writes,

> ... lust
> Is perjur'd, murderous, bloody, full of blame,
> Savage, extreme, rude, cruel, not to trust. ...

It is hortatory rather than persuasive, and there is some sacrifice of power to the exigencies of art. The anticlimactic position of "not to trust" is owing entirely to the need for a rime. But he does not make the sacrifice as often as in the earlier sonnets. He had no sooner mastered the homeliness than he employed it concretely and compactly to give immediacy— the constable, for instance, as the emblem of death:

> ... when that fell arrest
> Without all bail shall carry me away. ...

To us this vivid immediacy of the commonplace is not always as noticeable as it should be, since the dissonance of one age mellows into the harmony of the next. Time bestows

[27] Sonnet 129.

a patina; an image used successfully in a poem acquires poetic associations. But when Shakespeare's homely images were new they must have been as startling as Eliot's "patient etherized upon a table" seemed to be just a generation ago.

Shakespeare's use of this new and startling homeliness (could we call it the second major aspect of his style?) is of a piece with his juxtaposition of grandeur and horror. The juxtaposition of comedy and tragedy had long been a part of the English tradition, but it was reserved for Shakespeare to make each a part of the other; and we may see the growth of his poetic use of homeliness in the sonnets. There could be no purer instance of this development than the juxtaposition of styles in the seventy-third and seventy-fourth sonnets, two sonnets which comprise one poem. The first ("That time of year thou may'st in me behold") employs what had long been known to be the poetic image and the language of poetry. The second concentrates on the homely and the ugly and ends in a couplet of the barest language. There is not a word in the couplet (except perhaps *worth*) which carries an overtone. Language could not be more completely stripped of connotation. There is nothing to distract the reader from bare singleness of the thought. Yet the emotion of the quatrains carries over, and, in its context, the couplet is poetry. It is what he was later to do, perhaps more magnificently, with Lear's five *nevers*.

> But, be contented: when that fell arrest
> Without all bail shall carry me away,
> My life hath in this line some interest,
> Which for memorial still with thee shall stay.
> When thou reviewest this, thou dost review
> The very part was consecrate to thee:
> The earth can have but earth, which is his due;
> My spirit is thine, the better part of me:
> So then thou hast but lost the dregs of life,

The prey of worms, my body being dead,
The coward conquest of a wretch's knife,
Too base of thee to be remembered.
 The worth of that is that which it contains,
 And that is this, and this with thee remains.

The simplest statement of the sonnet's meaning would be, "the essential is best." It is an idea of which Shakespeare never wearied, and nothing more readily recalled its truth to him than the contemplation of poetry. He asks that the sonnets be remembered for their content.[28] He says that it is their subject that makes the poems pleasing, and not what the poet brings to them.[29] He repeats that his powers are not worthy of their theme. And once, after a long silence, he invoked his muse to return again to his friend and "sing to the ear that . . . gives thy pen both skill and argument."[30] The young friend, except for these poems, is now unknown, and Shakespeare has become the greatest of English writers. This admiration for a man we do not know, and this derogation of poetic powers we esteem, may strike us at first as curious. But the sonnets tell of a time when Shakespeare was unknown, or almost so, and the young man was not only well-known, he was, in the poet's eyes, fair, kind, and good. In those days the poet's attitude was not curious; and it is still less so when thought of in relation to his tendency to hold the subject more highly than the means by which it finds expression.

[28] Sonnet 32. [29] Sonnet 38. [30] Sonnet 100.

Shakespeare and the
Unromantic Lady

IN ONE of his plays Yeats asks, "If pleasure and remorse must both be there, which is the greater?" It is a question quite central to a consideration of Shakespeare's dark lady, for the sonnets devoted to her tell of an amour which began in pleasure and ended in moral loathing. Since remorse, for some time now, has been out of fashion in both literature and literary studies, the point of view expressed in these sonnets has not been taken very seriously. There has even been a tendency to deny its existence. It is true that the motivation of the remorse is complicated by the dark lady's liaison with Shakespeare's young friend, but that aspect of the matter can be reserved for other chapters without falsifying the central question. Besides, the pleasure and the remorse will provide more than enough material, for each is of a piece with the view of sex without romance disclosed throughout Shakespeare's works.

It should be stated in the beginning that this chapter assumes a certain order for the sonnets addressed to the poet's mistress. If the reader were to turn to an edition of the sonnets which reprints these poems, numbers 127 to 152, in their traditional order, he would be confronted with abrupt shifts from poem to poem. Invitations to love precede and follow rejections of it, and the anticipation of betrayal follows the betrayal itself. But if the sonnets are arranged in the order of the events of an ill-starred amour (compliments, invitations to love, consummation, joy, weariness, rejection) it will be found that the sonnets fall nicely into place and that no poem is left over. In Tucker Brooke's phrase, it is the order of their "psychological necessity."

There is nothing like the woman of Shakespeare's sonnets

in all the sonnet literature of the Renaissance. The ladies of
the sonnet tradition were idealizations; Shakespeare's heroine
represents neither the traditional ideal nor his. The Elizabethan ideal of beauty was blonde; Shakespeare's heroine,
if we may call her that, was dark, and the blackness of her
hair and eyes and heart is so heavily stressed that she has
come to be known as "the dark lady." He insists upon her
darkness—first the darkness of her beauty, and later the darkness of her deeds. But from the beginning, even when his
passion for her was untouched by regret, his praise of her
beauty was marked by ambivalence. It was perhaps the dominance of the traditional and popular ideal which made him
distrust the dictates of his senses. He opens the series with

> In the old age black was not counted fair,
> Or if it were, it bore not beauty's name.

But, he goes on to say, since nowadays the genuine beauty of
former times is recreated by cosmetics, true beauty is living
in disgrace, and your eyes have put on mourning for her;
therefore your eyes, having a true relation to beauty, are
beauty's legitimate successor. We notice that black is not the
real thing, or can be thought so only after some rationalization. To modern tastes the sonnet is overingenious, and the
compliment is oblique by any standards; yet the poem seems
to have been offered to the lady as a tribute, and it appears
that it could have been so received, for the woman is depicted
as free from illusion. Though she deceived others, she seems
not to have deceived herself. Sometimes the poet tells her
that her eyes are black because they know of her disdain
for him, that they have put on mourning in recognition of
his bondage to her. Whatever their context, Shakespeare's
compliments are always shadowed by his awareness of a discrepancy between the ideal and the fact, although there were
times when the fact did not seem to matter:

My mistress' eyes are nothing like the sun;
Coral is far more red than her lips' red:
If snow be white, why then her breasts are dun;
If hairs be wires, black wires grow on her head.
I have seen roses damask'd red and white,
But no such roses see I in her cheeks;
And in some perfumes is there more delight
Than in the breath that from my mistress reeks.
I love to hear her speak, yet well I know
That music hath a far more pleasing sound:
I grant I never saw a goddess go;
My mistress, when she walks, treads on the ground:
    And yet, by heaven, I think my love as rare
    As any she belied with false compare.[1]

Aware of the ideal, he here declares himself in favor of alloyed reality. He does not say that he loves her in spite of her faults; he loves her faults and all.

Considered in itself, the sonnet is pure comedy, at least by Meredith's standard, which required that the possessor of the comic spirit see the ridiculous in those he loved without loving them less. The spirit of "My mistress' eyes" is the spirit in which Dogberry, Falstaff, and the whole world of lovable imperfections were created. In this sense the poem is the essence of comedy. But if the poem is read in the light of the sonnet tradition, it is also satire. If we would appreciate Shakespeare's complexity, we must realize that this is not an *either/or* matter. The sonnet is satire or comedy or both, depending on what the reader brings to it. The sonnet contains them both, the only variable being the reader's ability to see. In this respect the sonnet is like the greater part of Shakespeare's work—hardly ever simple, hardly ever exhausted at one level of meaning. The reader of Shakespeare's day who had the slightest acquaintance with modern poetry

[1] Sonnet 130.

could not have missed the satire on the heroine of the sonnet tradition. She was the Renaissance descendant of chivalric love. Catullus and Ovid could not have imagined her, and Shakespeare could not take her seriously, though she was everywhere about him—in books, that is.

It is not necessary to consider the origins of the sonnet— Dante's use of it or its appearance in Provençal poetry. It is enough to say that Petrarch (1304-1374) fixed its form and content in the public mind and gave them currency. Petrarch's sonnets were written to Laura, who may or may not have been married when he first encountered her. Questions of her historic reality are not to the point, which is that during the greater part of his sonnets she appears as the loyal wife of another, and that the dominant characteristic of Petrarch's love is therefore its hopelessness. The hopelessness of Shakespeare's love is another matter. He despairs of his lady because there is no loyalty in her. She is, he remarks in nautical terms, "the bay where all men ride." But Petrarch's lady was unassailable, and his soul was overwhelmed with sadness. Loving her and knowing himself beneath her by virtue of her goodness, he idealized her and loved his idealization all the more. It was a situation which called forth the best uses of his poetic talents, creating for him an eminence from which he dominated the sonnet tradition for three centuries.

The kinds of experience to which Petrarch gave expression were those which Shakespeare also understood, but nowhere in his works does he regard them in isolation. Although an understanding of *Romeo and Juliet* assumes that under the depicted circumstances love is worth dying for, the love is not idealized to the point of irrelevance to actual life. It does not deny the body. Let Shakespeare's romance soar as high as it will, it is anchored in earth. The love always seems achievable, and partly because of the very human characteristics of his women in love. The qualities may be purer, more intense than in the work-a-day world, and sometimes, as in Cleopatra, they are innumerable. We might find a few of her qualities (less deeply felt, to be sure) anywhere, but she is the aggregate of infinite qualities of earth-dwelling womanhood.

The lady of the sonnet tradition may be a virgin, or she may be married, though not to the poet; but in either case her chief characteristic is her indomitable chastity. The lover professes his passion and devotion; she treats him with long disdain, and it is her fate to be taken at her word. She is "cruel" and "tyrannous" because she will not yield, a quality which drove Ronsard to the words "tigress" and "Medusa" and inspired a more homely epithet in the English Wyatt—"old mule." But these are passing irritations; the dominant tone is one of ardor and submission. The poet of the traditional sonnet often feels in his heart that his love is wrong, and he sometimes argues against himself on the side of morality— an understandable consequence of his towering idealization of the lady. One feels sometimes that nothing would disconcert him more than the sudden success of his suit, so dainty sweet is melancholy. There are, of course, exceptions: Spenser's *Amoretti* is the prologue to a marriage hymn. But the exceptions serve chiefly to emphasize the generality. The poet addresses the lady in terms of fire and ice (he is the fire, she the ice), of earth and air. He longs to touch her hand; he cherishes the glove that she has dropped. And so on! With Shakespeare, however, the essence of love is mutuality. With almost all the others the lover's condition is compared to a wrecked ship; with many the lady's hair is a golden net in which the lover is ensnared. He is desolate and sleepless, and his sighs trouble the heavens. The lady is described in terms of flowers, jewels, and all precious things. Her hair is threads of beaten gold, her forehead crystal, her eyes suns, her cheeks roses, her teeth pearls, her neck ivory or alabaster. Her features are detailed in what has come to be called the descending description. The poet begins with her hair and is restrained only by the limits of his ingenuity and the happy brevity of the sonnet form.

Sonnet number thirty-nine from the *Fidessa* of Bartholomew Griffin will provide an instance of the idle repetition of traditional formula. Griffin brings nothing to the tradition but the power to repeat, and the originality of his couplet, which is worse than nothing:

> My lady's hair is threads of beaten gold,
> Her front the purest crystal eye hath seen,
> Her eyes the brightest stars the heavens hold,
> Her cheeks red roses such as seld have been;
> Her pretty lips of red vermilion dye,
> Her hand of ivory the purest white,
> Her blush Aurora or the morning sky,
> Her breast displays two silver fountains bright,
> The spheres her voice, her grace the graces three:
> Her body is the saint that I adore;
> Her smiles and favors sweet as honey be;
> Her feet fair Thetis praiseth evermore.
> > But ah, the worst and last is yet behind,
> > For of a griffon doth she bear the mind.

It is not the failure of the sensibility which the couplet displays; it is the absence of it. Only when he is considered historically may Griffin be thought a part of the sonnet tradition. He repeats but he does not contribute. He is sub-literary. The weaknesses of Shakespeare's sonnets are often most striking in his couplets, but he has nothing like this. Nor is there anything in Shakespeare quite like the lapses of Sidney in, say, one of the four sonnets "made when his ladie had paine in her face." The basic conceit is that the poet had praised his lady's beauty so ardently that pain, enamored of her face, had gone to dwell there:

> Wo, wo, to me, on me return the smart:
> My burning tongue hath bred my mistress pain,

For oft in pain to pain my painful heart
With her due praise did of my state complain.
I prais'd her eyes whom never chance doth move,
Her breath which makes a sour answer sweet,
Her milken breasts the nurse of child-like love,
Her legs (O legs) her ay well stepping feet. . . .

From excesses like this, Shakespeare was saved by many things; for instance, his sense of comedy—the awareness of the ridiculous in those nearest him, and in himself. His failures were not, and could not have been, those which proceed from a solemn singleness of observation and intent.

In all truth there is very little in the dark lady sonnets which fails. The reader may dislike the punning "Will" sonnets, but once he sees through their complexity, it will be clear that they are brilliant examples of a departed fashion. Nor will he find that the virtuosity, once it is admitted, is unsuited to their subject—a laughing invitation to love. It turned out that Shakespeare's passion for the dark lady found its only joyous expression in comedy and word-play:

When my love swears that she is made of truth,
I do believe her though I know she lies,
That she might think me some untutor'd youth,
Unlearned in the world's false subtleties.
Thus vainly thinking that she thinks me young,
Although she knows my days are past the best,
Simply I credit her false speaking tongue:
On both sides thus is simple truth suppress'd.
But wherefore says she not she is unjust?
And wherefore say not I that I am old?
O, love's best habit is in seeming trust,
And age in love loves not to have years told:
　　Therefore I lie with her, and she with me,
　　And in our faults by lies we flatter'd be.[2]

[2] Sonnet 138.

Only a few of the twenty-six poems to the dark lady are in this mood of amused contentment.

Before long there were regrets, a deepening seriousness that made the lover think of his love as lust. When the seven deadly sins, recognized for what they are, have been given their proper names, the moral struggle has been defined, and everyone is on familiar ground; earlier, vision is not so clear. Of the time before realization the poet writes, "Love is too young to know what conscience is," using the word "conscience" in the double sense of "awareness" and "awareness of wrongdoing." Yet, he goes on to ask, who is there who does not know that conscience, in the second sense, is born of love? In this question, which the poet asks in passing, he glances at one of his most favored themes—the contribution of experience to moral knowledge. He was later to be more deeply concerned with the question, but in the sonnet under consideration[3] he goes on quickly to assert:

> My soul doth tell my body that he may
> Triumph in love; flesh stays no farther reason,
> But, rising at thy name, doth point out thee. . . .

At first glance the reader supposes that the lines of the sonnet which follow cannot be as frank as they seem to be; but they are, and the more one considers the lines, the more insistent their frankness becomes. The point is that the poet's relationship with the dark lady is neither dignified nor prettified; there is not a glimmer of romance. Later the relationship is considered and rejected, but for the time being it simply *is*. It is only one aspect of Shakespeare's view of love, but one that is characteristic of him, and quite uncharacteristic of literature in English as a whole, especially of the literature of our time. One thinks of Joyce's attitude toward Molly Bloom, and of very little else. In Steinbeck women of this sort are sentimentalized. In Hemingway love is essentially

[3] Sonnet 151.

romantic, a fictional presentation of man's age-old dream of a fuller and more carefree realization of his desires. There is a suave defiance in Sadie Thompson, an unstated turning of the tables. Anna Christie is washed clean by the sea. With still other writers, women like the dark lady become symbols. But not with Shakespeare! With him they are women first. We think of them as human beings; afterwards we recall their attributes.

Doll Tearsheet, the girl on call at Mistress Quickly's tavern, is so minor a character that everything she says and everything which is said about her could be printed on a page or two. Commentators and actresses alike prefer to think of her as pure trollop, thus simplifying the act of comprehension and making the task of the actress easier than Shakespeare intended it to be. I hope that I do not seem to bestow on Doll Tearsheet any considerable dignity. She is, of course, the most common of mortals; but she is not simply a type. Shakespeare establishes her commonness in the beginning. "What pagan may that be?"[4] asks the Prince when she is first mentioned. And the Page replies, "A proper gentlewoman, sir; and a kinswoman of my master's." The Prince is not deceived: "Even such kin as the parish heifers are to the town bull." Nothing that follows belies the guess, and the estimate of her character is confirmed on her first entrance, made after having drunk too much canary, "a marvelous searching wine" which "perfumes the blood e're one can say, 'What's this?'" Her conversation demonstrates that in all truth she is as "common as the way between St. Alban's and London." Shakespeare never pampers her. When we last see her she is being dragged off to prison for being what she is. Nor does he patronize her. He allows her a kind of wit and abundant animal spirits (the whore in modern literature is generally anemic) and although her tact is not what it should be, she means well: "I'll be friends with thee, Jack: thou

King Henry the Fourth, part two, 2.2.168.

art going to the wars; and whether I shall ever see thee again or no, there is nobody cares."[5] It is comedy, but it is not farce. There is a humanity which the actress would do well to remember. Shakespeare's feeling for Doll is written in the lines. It cannot be abstracted, and it must not be ignored. She is the embodiment of warm and tawdry humanity, and she is *also* a trollop. If in our love of categories we think of her as only a trollop and fail to distinguish her from her sisters, we shall reduce Shakespeare's sketch to a stereotype.

There is no word for the point of view embodied here. "Rabelaisian" will not do, for the gusto it implies suggests a commitment absent from Shakespeare. "Elizabethan" and "Shakespearean" indicate but do not define the view so free from both bravado and apology. Sometimes we read that Shakespeare's view is naïve, but nothing could be further from the truth. Shakespeare is not naïve; it is simply that he is not sophisticated. He is not afraid of the commonplace, and he can accept the simple without condescension. In one of his sonnets[6] he lists the things which displease him most, and among them he places "simple truth miscall'd simplicity." He is not Olympian, though no writer ever had more reason to be. He is not neutral. One understands the temptation to find him so, but it will not do. No writer's view of life was ever less a priori than Shakespeare's. He came to conclusions about life, but first he saw it. And what is more remarkable is that there are so many areas of his observation which his point of view does little to color. His tenderness does not trap him into sentimentality; his wit never serves as protective coloring, sophisticating the thrust of emotion to an easy obliquity. In the sonnets to the dark lady he accepts the passion, and, later, the remorse. "Everyone," wrote Aldous Huxley long ago when his wit was without solemnity, "feels a little Christian now and then, especially after an orgy." This is precisely the sort of awareness Shakespeare

[5] *Ibid.*, 2.4.71. [6] Sonnet 66.

did *not* have; it diminishes both the Christianity and the orgy. One of the greatest aspects of Shakespeare's art (no other writer has it to a like degree) is his ability to give us contrasting things without the slightest diminution of either. It was a gift which found its fullest expression in *Antony and Cleopatra.*

Someone has suggested that Shakespeare's recollection of the dark lady served as a basis for his characterization of Cleopatra. Clearly we cannot know; yet we might look at the basic conception. "Would I had never known her," said Antony early in the play when the storms had begun to gather. And Enobarbus replied, "Then you had left unseen a wonderful piece of work, which, not to have been blessed withal, would have discredited your travel."[7] This is more than an expression of Enobarbus' wit; it is the witty expression of a basic attitude. Although the imprudence of knowing Cleopatra is not denied, it is recognized that prudence is not all. Nor, on the other hand, is love. Nor is the moral judgment either denied or depreciated. Nor is either the scene or the play amoral. What is being established in this scene is the nature of Antony's love, for which, eventually, he will lose the world. The world, on the other hand, is not well lost. In Shakespeare's view of Antony's love there is greatness *and* wrong.

Both Antony and Cleopatra are mature and experienced people who have passed beyond romance. Having much in common besides sex, they recognize the basically sexual nature of their attachment with the same clarity and in much the same spirit as that in which Shakespeare recognizes the nature of his attachment to the dark lady. Cleopatra envies the horse that bears Antony's weight and takes "no pleasure in aught an eunuch has." Shakespeare addressed the dark lady with the same cruel frankness Antony used toward Cleopatra: "I found you as a morsel cold upon dead Caesar's

[7] *Antony and Cleopatra*, 1.2.161.

trencher." It seems to be difficult for the patterned mind to comprehend vulgarity in greatness, and the expression of it is a trying assignment for the actor. In her production of the play Miss Cornell, I thought, was magnificently regal, but at the cost of some of the coarseness. I am certain that if one is forced to a choice, Miss Cornell's choice was the right one, for I had seen the recent productions at Stratford and Paris which abandoned the queenliness altogether. As Maecenas (or was it Agrippa?) remarked in the barge scene at Paris, "Quel type!" The phrase did not matter; what mattered was the cliché of the mind to which Shakespeare's character had been reduced long before the phrase was spoken. This reduction of Shakespeare to a simplicity with which, because it is our simplicity, we can live in comfort, is the easy and common way of understanding him.

That Shakespeare should represent either Antony or himself as enslaved by sex is unpalatable to the Anglo-American tradition, which likes to have a good share of romance in the mythology by which it lives. Perhaps "Anglo-American" is not the phrase, but it will serve for something that is both English and American. Our spokesman is Hamlet in his antic disposition ". . . all which, sir, though I most powerfully and potently believe, yet I hold it not honesty to have it thus set down." Shakespeare's honesty allowed him to set down most unflattering views of mankind. On the night of the fulfillment of his love, young Troilus, fearful of going further, stands at his lady's door and engages her in forty lines of conversation: "This is the monstruosity in love, lady, that the will is infinite, and the execution confined; that the desire is boundless, and the act a slave to limit."[8] It is not an aspect of love which men often talk about together when talking about themselves. The lover may doubt, but it is not cricket to doubt himself. It is the kind of scene one might find in a French movie, but nothing like it has ever come out of

[8] *Troilus and Cressida*, 3.2.87.

Hollywood, where they know what the English-speaking public thinks it wants. Shakespeare gave his public both what they wanted and what he found true. Often they were the same thing, but what if they were not? Could there be more reason for sparing them than himself? His portrait as he has drawn it in the sonnets is not flattering. He presents himself as enslaved, and at times he is both witty and vulgar about it.

Away from his lady he imagines her faithless with his friend. Perhaps she is "wooing" the friend's "purity with her foul pride,"

> And whether that my angel be turned fiend,
> Suspect I may, yet not directly tell;
> But being both from me, both to each friend,
> I guess one angel in another's hell. . . .[9]

The reference is to that story in *The Decameron* usually left in Italian. In the edition before me it is printed in archaic French. Both Shakespeare's public and printers were more hearty and could face such matters. Indeed the heartiness of his public is so insisted upon nowadays that one is free to gather that Shakespeare indulged in vulgarity solely to please his public. This tactfully suggests that Shakespeare and his readers are above vulgarity, and thus everyone is left on the side of the angels except the people for whom he wrote. The truth is that Shakespeare had as fine a taste for the off-color remark as Queen Elizabeth and that between them they shared as much sensibility and Norman blood as a whole theaterful of others. If the reader approaches Shakespeare with the courage of his own vulgarity, he need not be troubled; and if he cannot bring himself to do so, he had better stick to Trollope. Shakespeare's vulgarity is a part of his view of life, and almost always it is an integral part of the work in which it appears.

[9] Sonnet 144.

Shakespeare's sketch of the dark lady is of a piece with the view of sex without romance revealed throughout his works. He regards it in turn with humor, contentment, rebellion, and revulsion—but never simply or falsely. His view here is no less manifold than his view of life as a whole. The woman is depicted as younger than he—how much younger we cannot know. He seems to have been about thirty when the sonnets were written, and he no doubt felt older. Perhaps there is no age except the last when one feels older than at thirty. When a man is in his twenties he can think of himself as a promising young man, but if he has any sense at all he cannot persuade himself that young manhood extends to the thirties. Our knowledge of Shakespeare indicates that he matured early. Such friends of his youth as we know anything about were older than he. He married at eighteen and was soon a father. By his thirtieth year he had been working in London for some time, and without the success that had come to Marlowe. His oldest child was nearing womanhood. He was old enough to feel older than he was, but not too old to pretend to be an "untutored youth." With his gift of comic self-awareness he magnified his age.

We may guess that the young woman was in her early twenties. She was married, faithless to her husband in her liaison with the poet, and faithless to them both in her affairs with others. She had "robb'd others' beds' revenues of their rents."[10] And he cannot understand why he thinks her a "several [that is, private] plot" while his heart knows her to be the "wide world's common place."[11] She is the "usurer that put'st forth all to use."[12] In varying moods of reproach he refers to her "unworthiness"[13] and calls her a "cheater,"[14] "covetous,"[15] and "unjust."[16] The ladies of the sonnet tradition were cruel in their chaste denials; the dark lady is cruel because she is gaily promiscuous while enforcing his bondage

---

[10] Sonnet 142. [11] Sonnet 137. [12] Sonnet 134.
[13] Sonnet 150. [14] Sonnet 151. [15] Sonnet 134.
[16] Sonnet 138.

<u>to her</u>. To this attitude (enslavement to a woman one recognizes as unworthy) the old conceit of the conflict between the eye and the heart is appropriate. Shakespeare might have found a fresher one, but it was his habit to use what was at hand when it would do.

The sonnets ask why the heart should be bound by what the eye can see is worthless. The question repeats, and the answer, when it comes, is as familiar as the question: although everyone knows that lust is

> perjur'd, murderous, bloody, full of blame. . . .
> none knows well
> To shun the heaven that leads men to this hell.[17]

Helpless in the grip of passion, he submits to her, forsaking his better self, trying at times to persuade himself that she is better than he knows her to be. He asks her to end the affair by saying that she does not love him, or, in his company, to let it appear that she does. And when it is clear that she will not be true, he begs her in a sonnet of extraordinary plainness to go her way and come back to him later. At first sight "feather'd creatures" for "chickens" looks like eighteenth-century poetic diction, but it is not an elegant evasion of the commonplace. It is intended to suggest a specious modishness in the successful rival:

> Lo, as a careful housewife runs to catch
> One of her feather'd creatures broke away,
> Sets down her babe, and makes all swift dispatch
> In pursuit of the thing she would have stay;
> Whilst her neglected child holds her in chase,
> Cries to catch her whose busy care is bent
> To follow that which flies before her face,
> Not prizing her poor infant's discontent:
> So run'st thou after that which flies from thee,
> Whilst I thy babe chase thee afar behind;

[17] Sonnet 129.

> But if thou catch thy hope, turn back to me,
> And play the mother's part, kiss me, be kind.... [18]

If in our admiration for Shakespeare we do not like to think of his playing this role, we should remember that this is his own sketch. If we gloss over the matter, preferring to understand it in another sense, we shall only contribute to the current puzzlement at his reputed rejection of love in favor of friendship; but if we take Shakespeare at his word, seeing the love as he asks us to see it, his ultimate choice is not only clear, it is inevitable.

Although the view of love depicted in the sonnets is a partial one, it accords with the larger view disclosed in his works as a whole. It will do no harm to say that the concept is romantic if we will remember that it is also classical, that it is, in fact, as old as literature. It regards love as a wild plant which may very well flourish in ordered gardens, but whose nature urges it always to its original state. In Shakespeare's most charming and lighthearted love story, Cupid once shot a shaft that, missing its mark, fell by chance upon a little flower, "before milk-white, now purple with love's wound...."

> The juice of it on sleeping eyelids laid
> Will make or man or woman madly dote.... [19]

The juice is applied by Puck at the behest of Oberon upon the eyelids of sleeping mortals who have no choice in the matter, and "Lord, what fools these mortals be!" Throughout his works Shakespeare expresses this view of love in different moods and terms and to different ends, but it is the same concept. Though the concept increased in content with his maturity, it was his from the beginning. It is basic to the love of Romeo, the passion of Antony, and that of the poet for the dark lady. The same concept centuries ago created Aphro-

[18] Sonnet 143.
[19] *A Midsummer Night's Dream*, 2.1.167.

dite to symbolize the willful and irrational dominance of passion.

In the sonnets Shakespeare writes that his eyes do not find the lady beautiful, that his ears are not delighted with her voice, and that

> Nor taste nor smell desire to be invited
> To any sensual feast with thee alone;
> But my five wits nor my five senses can
> Dissuade one foolish heart from serving thee. . . .[20]

It is the same simultaneousness of attraction and revulsion which was to become so characteristic of his dramatic treatment of sex in later years.

This is a complexity which has often been misconstrued, especially in our own age; for although modern writers are often unsentimental and antiromantic, they have accustomed us to a treatment of sex essentially different from Shakespeare's. Generally the reader views the anti-eroticism of, say, Eliot's poetry abstractly. It is not presented in a context of well-rounded characters and it remains to an extent disassociated from the life we live. Although the context of Eugene O'Neill's treatment of sex gives it immediacy, we accept it in spite of its unattractiveness because the temper of the time has prepared us for it. In none of O'Neill's major plays is an important sexual relationship viewed as satisfactory. Passion dominates and tortures, but it brings neither contentment nor release. This is acceptable to our time because the popularizations of modern psychology have provided patterns by which it can be interpreted. In O'Neill's major plays, except *The Iceman Cometh*, passion deviates from the normal. The strongest sexual drives are diverted by mother-son, father-daughter, or brother-sister attractions. Thus the unhappiness of passion is both presented and accepted as the manifestation of neurosis. With Shakespeare

[20] Sonnet 141.

this is not the case. The unhappiness is presented in itself as a commonly observed aspect of life. The passion which dominates and tortures is thought of as a manifestation of man's natural self. The view of human nature is not optimistic; there are *at once* incalculable potentials for both good and evil. This was and is the orthodox Christian view (it is also, among other things, Platonic), but there seems to be no great popular awareness of it; and it is clearly not the assumption on which the average English-speaking spectator responds to a dramatic situation. Nor has it been for some time! "It is now quite unfashionable," wrote John Wesley,[21] "to say anything to the disparagement of human nature; which is generally allowed, notwithstanding a few infirmities, to be very innocent, and wise, and virtuous." In the popular view what is evil in man is thought of as a deviation from a goodness he once possessed. Generally, even in our most robust fiction, the evil in man is in a sense man-made. Its social and neurotic origins are commonly explained, and the most terrifying aspect of evil is thus explained away. This is what the average reader has come to expect of literature, and not finding it in Shakespeare, he often reads it into the text. Shakespeare's works assume the reality of both good and evil, and while it is once or twice suggested that a certain trait of character is the result of training (the only notable instance is Coriolanus) sexual evil is never presented as the manifestation of a neurosis.

I do not of course mean to suggest that tragic suffering in both literature and life does not often have social or psychiatric origins. I simply remark that Shakespeare's assumptions in this respect are not ours and that we both obscure and diminish his work in trying to make his assumptions conform to our own. It is no objection to Freud to observe that in almost all instances the Freudian interpretations of Shake-

[21] Quoted by Louis A. Landa, *English Institute Essays, 1946*, Columbia University Press, New York, 1947, p. 34.

speare have done him an injustice; but in order to have written more wisely the Freudian critics would have needed little but a more complete knowledge of Freud, who knew quite well that Shakespeare had preceded him in observing certain phenomena. Both of them knew that a sense of revulsion in erotic life is not necessarily either neurotic or puritanical. There is at least one passage in which Freud out-Shakespeares Shakespeare[22]: "So perhaps we must make up our minds to the idea that altogether it is not possible for the claims of the sexual instinct to be reconciled with the demands of culture. . . . This very incapacity in the sexual instinct to yield full satisfaction as soon as it submits to the first demands of culture becomes the source, however, of the grandest cultural achievements, which are brought to birth by ever greater sublimation of the components of the sexual instinct. For what motive would induce man to put his sexual energy to other uses if by any disposal of it he could obtain fully satisfying pleasure? . . . It seems, therefore, that the irreconcilable antagonism between the demands of the two instincts—the sexual and the egoistic—have made man capable of ever greater achievements, though, it is true, under the continual menace of danger, such as that of the neuroses to which at the present time the weaker are succumbing." We may believe that Shakespeare was not one of "the weaker" who succumbed, but that, since he was a man of strong passion and fine sensibility, the conflict between the claims of sex and his integrity as a civilized man were most apparent to him. It was inevitable that as a man of his time he should express the conflict in terms of body and soul, and that, when the expression pierces to ultimates, the point of view should be Christian.

This conflict is the essence of the later sonnets to the dark lady, and it is, of course, central to *Hamlet*, where it is nowhere better set forth than in Hamlet's excoriation of his

[22] *Freud: On War, Sex and Neurosis*, Arts & Science Press, New York, 1947, pp. 216-217.

mother. We should notice in passing that here again there is the opposition of the eyes and the heart:

> Have you eyes?
> Could you on this fair mountain leave to feed,
> And batten on this moor? Ha! Have you eyes?

On the basis of his own experience Hamlet understands the power of passion, but as a young man he cannot believe that it can so operate in his mother without infernal aid. There is, of course, a double value here: the revelation of particular character and the suggestion to the spectator of motives arising in realms beyond human control.

> . . . at your age
> The hey-day in the blood is tame, it's humble,
> And waits upon the judgment; and what judgment
> Would step from this to this. . . . What devil was't
> That thus hath cozen'd you. . . .

The dramatic fact is that the judgment had not functioned. The queen is not presented as a villainess for our scorn and hatred. The more fortunate of us may say of her, "There but for the grace of God go I." Up to this point in the play she had not recognized the enormity of her actions; she had never had the courage to look into her soul. Hamlet now forces self-knowledge upon her, and in her soul she sees

> such black and grained spots
> As will not leave their tinct.

Terrified at the realization of what she is, she tries to escape it. If, after all, her son should be mad, his revelation of her nature would be without reality. She prefers his madness, but it will not serve:

> Mother, for love of grace,
> Lay not that flattering unction to your soul,
> That not your trespass but my madness speaks;
> It will but skin and film the ulcerous place

While rank corruption, mining all within,
Infects unseen. Confess yourself to Heaven;
Repent what's past, avoid what is to come,
And do not spread the compost on the weeds
To make them ranker.

No scene in dramatic literature is more deeply revealing or more theatrically varied. The recognition of lust moves with a speed it could not have in the sonnets—yet it is the same recognition, moving to the same conclusion with the same tearing back of surfaces.

For the moment we should note that in representing his uneasiness in the adulterous relationship, Shakespeare refers repeatedly to his being forsworn; that is, to the breaking of his vows, to the denial of his integrity. And if we glance again at the list of wrongs which, in sonnet sixty-six, make him in his weariness cry for "restful death," we shall find among them "purest faith unhappily forsworn." We should notice, too, that the sonnets depict a progress on the poet's part which is parallel to the spiritual progress of Lear. Lear's journey from arrogance to a knowledge of his own unworthiness shows, near the beginning, an attempt to lighten the growing burden by the assertion that although he has erred, the wrongs of others are greater: "I am a man more sinned against than sinning." In the sonnets the poet repeats that although he is forsworn, the lady is twice forsworn. Can she condemn him when her errors are more than his? This is a familiar attempt at the maintenance of illusion, but in Shakespeare it does not work. Their rationalizations failing, both Lear and Gertrude move on to self-knowledge. The poet of the sonnets comes to think of his love as a thing without health, as a fever always longing "for that which longer nurseth the disease." He comes to loathe his passion, and his loathing swells until it includes both himself and the dark lady:

For I have sworn thee fair and thought thee bright,
Who art as black as hell, as dark as night.[23]

The sonnets of deepest revulsion present an agony which
cannot contain itself. One thinks of the writers of our own
day—the desolation of *The Wasteland*, of the earlier novels
by Huxley and their searing wit without the release of indignation. It is an awareness which must change because
it cannot bear to be itself. With Shakespeare it moved to
a magnification of the spirit and a renunciation of the flesh,
set forth in a sonnet[24] of admirable compactness and, once
the precision of its grammatical references are noticed, of
perfect clarity:

Poor soul, the center of my sinful earth,
Thrall to[25] these rebel powers that thee array,
Why dost thou pine within and suffer dearth,
Painting thy outward walls so costly gay?
Why so large cost, having so short a lease,
Dost thou upon thy fading mansion spend?
Shall worms, inheritors of this excess,
Eat up thy charge? is this thy body's end?
Then soul, live thou upon thy servant's loss,
And let that pine to aggravate thy store;
Buy terms divine in selling hours of dross;
Within be fed, without be rich no more:
So shalt thou feed on death, that feeds on men,
And death once dead, there's no more dying then.

There is nothing with which the sonnets are more insist-
ently concerned than with the aspiration to triumph over
death. In the early sonnets immortality is to be won through
propagation and poetry. At the close it is to be found in the
salvation of the soul. Throughout there is a progressive

---

[23] Sonnet 147.   [24] Sonnet 146.
[25] "Thrall to" is a widely accepted conjectural emendation. In the
original text the line begins with a manifest error.

growth in moral emphasis. I do not suggest, of course, that the sonnets are primarily a sequence of moral poems; and it should be pointed out that although the recognition of lust extends over many poems, there is only one poem which renounces the flesh. Still, the poem exists and seems to be the culmination of the sonnets to the dark lady. I can see no possible basis of agreement with the critic who does not believe that in this sonnet "Shakespeare is making out a case for immortality except as a formal device." What is there in all of Shakespeare's works, or in his background, which would lead us to suppose that when he speaks of the immortality of the soul he is "making out a case" for it?

Although the dominant mode of criticism in our time insists on the necessity of viewing a work of literature in relation to its historical background, certain predispositions of our own century have prevented modern criticism from recognizing so patent a matter as the essential nature of this poem. One may read all the commentaries on this sonnet in the New Variorum and hardly discover a centrally relevant remark. One summer evening not so many years ago, five critics gathered in a kind of symposium at The Bread Loaf School of English to discuss this poem. The meeting was without wine or auditors, although, in deference to one of their number, there were cigars. The conversation, as reported in *The American Scholar*,[26] was wonderfully sober in spite of a vein of fantasy arising, doubtless, from the privacy of the meeting. The remarkable thing about what was said is not that it was wrong-headed and learnedly foolish, for to be wrong and foolish a good part of the time is the normal state of mankind. The disturbing thing is that critics of distinction should have shown such fear of being plain. One of the critics, finding in himself a "tendency to take the images literally and seriously," saw " 'center' as per-

---

[26] *The American Scholar*, Vol. 12 (1943), "Critical Principles and a Sonnet," pp. 52-62.

haps the capital city of England and the 'rebel powers' as English Barons at the beginning of the 15th century." This is in spite of Shakespeare's warning that "they that dally nicely with words may quickly make them wanton." He continued, "Or I pause on the word 'array' to think of its connections with decoration and painting. 'Array' is a transitive verb and its use here is ambiguous. The rebel powers can array, or marshall, only their own troops—not the troops of the opposing soul."

Surely the less complicated reader will not be troubled in this way. He will notice that *thee* is the object of *array* and refers to the *poor soul* which is incarnated in the poet's flesh, his *sinful earth*. He will notice, too, that *excess* refers to the body, and he will not find that it "unescapably" suggests Aristotle's doctrine of the mean. It is the clear and completely appropriate word because, as the poem insists, the soul is immortal, and the flesh, being transient, has no essential value. It is excess impedimenta which we can carry only to the grave, where it will be consumed by worms. The notion of dissolution, as familiar in Shakespeare as it is in life, struck one of the Bread Loaf critics as "cannibalistic," the "imagery of the eating worms" being "so excessive as to destroy any calm ethical judgments in the argument." "Taken literally, the notions of these lines are horrid and to me very painful." These remarks are the expression of a sensibility so intent upon itself that it disregards the poem, except to distort it. Animals that prey upon each other, or upon carrion, do not suggest cannibalism to a more disengaged intelligence.

The ordinary reader reflecting on these remarks can only be shocked at the critic's refusal to turn his eyes from himself toward the object of criticism, and he could only be more deeply shocked at the degree to which contemporary criticism is compounded of such proud and private pedantry. Willfully private, in this instance, for the critic finds "few words in the poem that would directly indicate conventional religious dogma . . . the sonnet seems in spirit to be Platonic." Another member of the Bread Loaf symposium whose criticism is seldom far from center, finds that "the movement of the poem is ascetic." "Superficially, I suppose, we could call the doctrine Christian; it is conventional in its argument; it is almost sentimental in its doing away with the painful and the transient and the worthless, in its centering of man's hope upon immortality and a system of future rewards and punishments." This is better. Yet there is the horrid condescension to the subject matter of the poem, the feeling that there is something about Christianity a little unworthy of us, and certainly of Shakespeare. The feeling is strong enough to equate renunciation with asceticism and relegate it to the "movement" of the poem, allowing the critic to view it with the detachment one rightly accords to technical matters. And all this is representative of the greater part of the criticism of this sonnet. There is a reluctance to admit that Shakespeare means something; or, if a meaning is admitted, there is a refusal to view it simply. The criticism of this sonnet is on the whole a dismal record of the triumph of sophistication over sense.

"What strikes me particularly about this poem," said still another Bread Loaf critic, "is its tone. I find it jaunty, full of a kind of super-wit . . . in spite of this central mood of jauntiness, the opponents are the worms, the flesh, and the grave; therefore a certain grimness and irony are present." Surely it should be apparent to all men in their senses that although there is often wit in Shakespeare's seriousness, this is not a jaunty poem, that the poem is Christian, and that Shakespeare presents the Christianity without apology. The "opponents" are neither the worms nor the grave. The opponent is the inherent willfulness of the flesh, and the poem says that when sin is conquered death is conquered, for death has no power over the soul. There can be no error in seeing

Platonic relationships in the poem, for they exist; but it is blindness not to see that the poem is first Christian. If we must have a written source for the poem, it can be found in the most obvious of places, the words of Saint Paul: "O death, where is thy sting? O grave, where is thy victory? The sting of death is sin. . . ." The triumph here is that of the spirit over sin, and in the light of this triumph death takes on insignificance. No one supposes that all readers of Shakespeare will share this belief, but it is a little late to deny the use of it to Shakespeare. The exhortation to his soul to find eternal life in shattering his sexual enslavement is an understandable consequence of the passion he describes. It is a sequence noted in Huxley's epigram, and, much more wisely, by Saint Paul. "Howbeit that was not first which is spiritual, but that which is natural; and afterwards that which is spiritual."

Mutability, Plenitude, and Immortality

THROUGHOUT the long opening sequence of the sonnets, poems one through seventeen, Shakespeare urges his friend to marry and beget a child, arguing that propagation is a double duty—to the young man himself and to the world, for time which made him will destroy him, and without his progeny the world to come will not know what he was. A little later in the sequence the poet promises to immortalize the friend's youthful splendor in poetry, while assuring him that the bestowal of immortality in verse will not relax the need to breed:

> But wherefore do you not a mightier way
> Make war upon this bloody tyrant, Time?
> And fortify yourself in your decay
> With means more blessed than my barren rime?[1]

The section closes with the statement that if the friend were to have a child, he would live twice, "in it and in my rime."

It is often asked why Shakespeare should have bothered with so odd a subject as a friend's failure to have children. In our century one does not find that poets have been much concerned with the immortality of others, and I do not remember any who has expressed a belief in man's obligation to reproduce his kind. Far from it! Not only is the belief no longer current among literary people, it is often considered ridiculous to suppose that a sensible person should ever have held it seriously. "The preposterous theme," writes Thornton Wilder,[2] of "Go, young man, and get married

---

[1] Sonnet 16.

[2] Thornton Wilder, Preface to *Four in America*, Gertrude Stein, Yale University Press, New Haven, 1947, p. xxii.

in order that you may leave a copy of your excellences to the after-world." To others it is a meaningless notion which Shakespeare toyed with on an afternoon of idle singing—"an argument for Arcadia." To still others it is simply the repetition of a conventional theme—Shakespeare doing his duty by the fashion of his day. But when one remembers that Shakespeare's Arcadias were never far from London, that he had precious little time for idleness, was seldom foolish, and, I think, never preposterous, it seems reasonable to reflect a bit on his ideas before rejecting them. In another connection one of our best critics has said that there is something naïve in all Elizabethan art. It may be so! On the other hand, it may be that Shakespeare and his fellows were no more naïve than we are.

The reader who turns to the first seventeen sonnets will notice first of all the many unforgettable lines and phrases among others of less grace. He will also notice that two of the poems are among the best known in the language. He may wonder to what they owe their fame. Is it solely to their technical excellence or their verbal beauty? Or is there something in the content which the average reader finds worthy of acceptance, something on which he can reflect with an awareness of deepened perception? If this is the case, he may wonder about the relevance of his regard for the poems to this "preposterous" notion. Hardly an anthology to which the inclusion of poems by Shakespeare is appropriate fails to reprint the twelfth and fifteenth sonnets —"When I do count the clock that tells the time," and "When I consider everything that grows," the two sonnets almost always selected by students when asked to choose the best sonnets in the opening sequence. Although either would serve our purpose, we shall look at the fifteenth.

> When I consider everything that grows
> Holds in perfection but a little moment,

That this huge stage presenteth nought but shows
Whereon the stars in secret influence comment;
When I perceive that men as plants increase,
Cheer'd and check'd even by the selfsame sky,
Vaunt in their youthful sap, at height decrease,
And wear their brave state out of memory;
Then the conceit of this inconstant stay
Sets you most rich in youth before my sight,
Where wasteful time debateth with decay,
To change your day of youth to sullied night;
  And, all in war with time for love of you,
  As he takes from you, I engraft you new.

When the young reader is asked if he finds the poem equally impressive all the way through, he replies that he finds the couplet inferior, an impression he does not discard after the couplet's promise of immortality is made clear to him. He may find several reasons for preferring the quatrains, and one of them will be the generality of the thought. It is relevant to the poet, to the person to whom the sonnet is addressed, and to every reader. On the other hand the couplet is particular; it is addressed to the young man with at most the partial or incidental involvement of the reader. It is not the promise of immortality but the realization of mortality which impresses. One feels that its truth, its obviousness notwithstanding, has been genuinely perceived and poetically realized.

As everyone knows, the briefness of beauty and the consuming power of time are themes recurrent throughout Shakespeare's works; and one may surmise from the power of his expression of them in the early sonnets that they were deeply felt before the idea of opposing mutability with poetry had had any considerable emotional reality for him. In a short time Shakespeare was to be able to write with conviction about his poetic powers, but in the beginning the idea of opposing mutability with poetry seems to have been an emergent corollary to his vivid apprehension of decay. It would be natural for a young poet to be first impressed with the transience of bodily things; and it would be natural, too, that, as he matured and deepened, the emphasis of his concern with transience should shift. At least it was natural to Shakespeare.

In the sonnets the decay of beauty is observed with pain and rebellion, and sometimes with horror, as in the many passages on ultimate decay. In the early works generally, time is a villain because of his conquest of youth and beauty. In the later works, roughly after the turn of the century, this is not the case. For instance, in a well-known passage in *Troilus and Cressida* time's function is to feed the monster, Oblivion, with the good deeds of men,

> which are devour'd
> As fast as they are made, forgot as soon as done. . . .[3]

In the passage from *Troilus* the notion is related to a context to which an emphasis on beauty would not be appropriate. Still, the change is representative of his maturing; and even here he does not forget beauty, for we find it later in the speech, now only one of time's victims:

> For beauty, wit
> High birth, vigor of bone, desert in service,
> Love, friendship, charity, are subjects all
> To envious and calumniating Time. . . .

Shakespeare has not come to love beauty less; he has come to love other things as much—or so it seems. But in the early sonnets the emphasis falls upon the things a young man holds dearest, and the decay of beauty stirs his awakening powers more deeply than the promises of immortality. We need not conclude from this that the poet did not in general

[3] *Troilus and Cressida*, 3.3.148.

believe the arguments which strike us as comparatively lacking in vigor, or still less that in setting them forth he was
deliberately using themes he knew to be of little value. It
is rather that for a number of reasons, some of them technical
and others, no doubt, of the spirit, he was unable to find for
them the expression he sought. Would it be too subjective
a judgment to remark that in these poems the direct injunctions to breed come with less force, not only than the passages on immortality, but than the more general statements
of man's obligations to put to use the good qualities with
which he is graced?

> Unthrifty loveliness, why dost thou spend
> Upon thyself thy beauty's legacy?
> Nature's bequest gives nothing, but doth lend. . . .[4]

Is it too private a judgment to remark that early in his
career the particular injunctions suffered from the poet's inability to project his convictions into specific instances? Later,
as we have said, the promises of immortality were stated
with passion. In the meantime the injunctions had been
abandoned, though the general notion of the goodness of
propagation is to be found everywhere.

Perhaps no idea repeated by Shakespeare is more alien to
the modern temper. One gathers from the recurrent contro-
versies on birth control that while the Catholic Church does
not require propagation of its married members, it denies
them the freedom to prevent it. But as recent polls indicate,
there are many Catholics who do not receive the denial
cordially. It appears that in our time the most influential
agency advancing the ancient and orthodox doctrine of the
goodness of propagation meets with only partial success. It
is almost useless to look for the doctrine in secular areas.
Although the love of fecundity is to be found from time to
time in modern fiction, there is no considerable expression

[4] Sonnet 4.

of it in modern poetry. On the other hand, statements comparable to Hardy's *I Said to Love* are to be found everywhere. It will not be necessary to quote more than a stanza of the poem:

> Man's race shall perish, threatenest thou,
> Without thy kindling coupling-vow?
> The age to come the man of now
>   Know nothing of?
> We fear not such a threat from thee;
> We are too old in apathy!
> *Mankind shall cease*—"So let it be,"
> I said to love.

This is the view held by modern poetry, in so far as it may be said to have one; and it is a curious commentary on our times that critics accept it with no sense of strangeness while rejecting Shakespeare's view as specious.

As it appears in the sonnets, the idea is part of a complex of ideas from which it cannot be readily isolated. It is inextricably related to at least two things, an idea and an attitude, both highly characteristic of Shakespeare. The first is the idea of stewardship. Nothing is more basic to Shakespeare's thought than the conviction that a man has an obligation to nature, that he is the steward and not the owner of his qualities. The second is his attitude toward the physiological aspects of sex, which has been discussed earlier and to which we shall soon return. With them as a background, the admonition to propagate will appear less strange than in isolation.

At the close of *As They Liked It*, Professor Alfred Harbage discusses the attitude of Shakespeare's plays toward parenthood and remarks that "the characters seem to desire children simply because children are a good thing to have." He points to the cropping up of this desire in the plays, instances quite independent of their sources, and he finds the desire to be one of the things Shakespeare's works share with common people, who, even today, "are sad at the death of a child and joyful at the birth of a child, not having read those books urging that they be sad on both occasions." Shakespeare assigns the belief in the goodness of propagation impartially to his characters. It is urged by such diverse persons as the clown in *All's Well*,[5] Venus,[6] and the heroine of *Twelfth Night*[7]:

> Lady, you are the cruelest she alive,
> If you will lead these graces to the grave,
> And leave the world no copy.

Parenthood is presented not only as good but as urgent, and there is not the slightest suggestion that Shakespeare expected his audiences to consider it odd. Further, when the dialogue glances critically at virginity it is to note its barrenness—the "faint hymns,"[8] for instance, which the barren sisters, "in shady cloister mew'd," chant "to the cold, fruitless moon."

The truth is that the man of Shakespeare's day was heir to a tradition of plenitude which had not yet fallen into distrust or been diverted, as in our own time and country, toward manufactured things. It was as basic to the Elizabethan love of magnificence as to what we now in more than one sense consider Elizabethan vulgarity. There is neither the time nor the need to trace the history of the complex doctrine of plenitude, the more so since the growth of the philosophical arguments to which Shakespeare's notions are parallel is set forth in one of the best known studies of our time, Professor A. O. Lovejoy's *The Great Chain of Being*. The origins of the doctrines as disclosed there are more than sufficiently ancient and reputable for our purpose. They are the *Timaeus* of Plato and the *Physics* and *Metaphysics* of

[5] 1.1.131, ff.
[7] 1.5.259-261.
[6] *Venus and Adonis*, 750 ff.
[8] *A Midsummer Night's Dream*, 1.1.73.

Aristotle. It should be stated again that we refer to backgrounds, the sources from which, philosophically considered, Shakespeare's notions derived. Professor Lovejoy does not discuss Shakespeare, nor does the *Timaeus* accord a high place to human reproduction. Nor is it necessary for Shakespeare to have studied the neo-Platonists of his time. He is not a philosopher, except in the sense in which philosophy is, as with Plato, the love of wisdom. He came by his ideas in the common and manifold ways of the literate, intelligent, gregarious man. He could have picked up his ideas on propagation anywhere; they were both religiously and philosophically orthodox, and were a part, then as now, of the uninstructed wisdom of the common man.

They were also a part of Shakespeare's literary heritage, and they had been a part of it since the composition of *The Romance of the Rose* in the thirteenth century. *The Romance* is a long allegory of love, begun by Guillaume de Lorris and finished forty years later by Jean de Meun. It quickly became a most popular and influential book. "It is hardly an exaggeration to say that for two hundred years no important French author escaped its influence. In England its vogue was little less extensive. Without it Chaucer would not have been Chaucer, and English literature would have followed a different channel."[9] The poem won its phenomenal popularity because it "crystallized into masterful poetic expression a literary form and a set of ideas which were already current and popular."[10] Chaucer translated part of the poem into English and fell heavily under the influence of both its authors. Through Chaucer the attitudes of the poem gained currency in English letters, becoming easily available to all readers of English literature. A discursive poem of over twenty-two thousand lines, *The Romance of the Rose* has

[9] R. K. Root, *The Poetry of Chaucer*, Houghton Mifflin Company, The Riverside Press, Cambridge, 1922, p. 49.

[10] *Ibid.*, p. 50.

much to say, but we are here concerned with only one aspect of the second part of the poem, the view of love as, in Alan Gunn's phrase, "life's instrument in its race with death."

It seems to have been easier in the Middle Ages and the Renaissance to be concerned with the elemental and the essential. It was certainly so in the treatment of love. Although there was, as always, the need to formalize love (and the need is greater as the passion of the individual and the life of society are the more ferocious), the medieval formalizations, for all their intricate artifice, do not blind themselves to its physical aspects. *The Romance of the Rose*[11] presents the same arguments for propagation found in Shakespeare and the same attitudes toward generation and the generative organs which are their natural corollary. If a writer is deeply aware of the riches of the world, the joy of love, the splendor and briefness of beauty, and the terror of oblivion, he is not likely to think of the body with shyness, and he will find it good to have a child. If he lives in a society which feels as he does, he will have no reason, like many intellectuals of our own age, to think that he ought not to find it so. He will write as Shakespeare, Chaucer, Jean de Meun, and others did, and as few writers have done since. "It is unnecessary indeed," writes Professor Gunn,[12] ". . . to demonstrate Jean de Meun's appreciation of the surging tides of life. The richness and variety of his work, a richness and variety . . . which is reflected . . . in the ever-branching figures of his rhetoric; his sheer exuberance; his delight in everything that moves and lives . . . quite apart from any philosophical or theological doctrines in regard to the divine bounty—show him to be above all other writers of his day . . . the supreme celebrant of God's plenitude." There would be little change needed to

[11] See Chaucer's translation 4850 ff.
[12] Alan Gunn, *A Reinterpretation of the "Roman de la Rose,"* p. 408. I quote from the manuscript in the Princeton library. The book will be published shortly.

make this passage a description of Shakespeare, and that would be a matter of addition, for as it stands the passage does not suggest Shakespeare's tragic grandeur. Exuberance, though incompatible with solemnity, goes hand in hand with tragic seriousness—or at any rate it did when tragic seriousness was at its height.

A writer who shares the point of view of Jean de Meun will sometimes write with an openness for which in our restriction of spirit we have no word. "Phallicism" is a current makeshift, a wretched word which escapes the taint of puritanism only to create a cult of its own, leaving unindicated the heartiness of some of the sonnets as well as Shakespeare's laughing recognition, in the twentieth sonnet, of the harmony and happy difference between friendship and passion. Such a writer will not think that he is writing frankly, for frankness implies a certain resolution. He will not write with innocence, for innocence is without knowledge, and he is knowing. To him creation is of a piece, and it is—all of it—potentially good. In the eleventh sonnet Shakespeare associates "wisdom, beauty, and increase," and to them he opposes "folly, age, and cold decay." It is a point of view altogether characteristic. It emerges everywhere, sometimes even when it has little relevance to the dramatic situation or the character of the speaker. In *Measure for Measure* the dissolute and lively hedonist, Lucio, while on a visit to a convent announces Juliet's illegal pregnancy with,

> Your brother and his lover have embrac'd;
> As those that feed grow full, as blossoming time
> That from the seedness the bare fallow brings
> To teeming foison, even so her plenteous womb
> Expresseth his full tilth and husbandry.[13]

For the modern reader the association of begetting and husbandry may stress a pun, but for Shakespeare it was also

[13] I.4.40-44.

an ancient and just association of meanings and the recognition of an identity of function. Procreation is mentioned in terms of tilling and ploughing, and most often without grossness. It was Bowdler's unhappy way to remove these passages from his "family" Shakespeare. But that was in another century! In our own time the rejection of them is part of the self-consciousness of the literati, very few of whom, one hopes, are really bored with "birth and copulation and death," though many appear to feel they ought to be, and would, if they read *The Romance of the Rose*, agree with C. S. Lewis that the *significatio* of Jean de Meun is "hardly worth the finding." When he wanted to, Shakespeare could use fertility images with grossness, as in *Antony and Cleopatra*,[14] but the customary attitude is one of joy in abundance. In sharp distinction to many critics, the average man will find the advice to marry and get a child to be in general sound. Perhaps some of us find it unbecoming in Shakespeare, partly because for quite other reasons the benign role of leading our bachelor friends to the fuller life is seldom a gracious one and is hardly ever played without a touch of gaucherie. Still, there never was a married person who could resist the role, and it ought not to be thought strange that Shakespeare, with the total tradition behind him, should have played it too.

Both in itself and its corollary attitudes, the point of view disclosed by Shakespeare's advice is remarkably like some notions we may read elsewhere. In explaining that love is not simply the love of beauty, Diotima said that it was also "the love of generation and of birth in beauty . . . because to the mortal creature generation is a sort of eternity and immortality. . . . Marvel not, she said, if you believe that love is of the immortal . . . for . . . the mortal nature is seeking as far as possible to be everlasting and immortal: and this is to be attained only by generation, because generation always leaves

---

[14] For example, 2.2.233.

behind a new existence in the place of the old ... the old worn
out mortality leaving another new and similar existence behind—unlike the divine, which is always the same and not
another. In this way, Socrates, the mortal body ... partakes
of immortality. ..."[15]

In the fifth sonnet our mortal partaking of immortality is
expressed through the erotic image of distillation. If left to
itself, the flower (beauty's rose of the first sonnet) will die
with the coming of winter; but if it is distilled to perfume
it shall have lost only its "show" (that is, the physical nature
by which it is manifest), and its "substance"[16] will continue
in essential sweetness:

> Then, were not summer's distillation left,
> A liquid prisoner pent in walls of glass,
> Beauty's effect with beauty were bereft,
> Nor it, nor no remembrance what it was:
> But flowers distill'd, though they with winter meet,
> Leese but their show, their substance still lives sweet.

The theme is continued in the following poem:

> Then let not winter's ragged hand deface
> In thee thy summer, ere thou be distill'd:
> Make sweet some vial; treasure thou some place
> With beauty's treasure, ere it be self-kill'd.

There could not be more successful writing. The value of
the erotic image of the vial is immediately apparent without
the slightest obtrusion of its physiological nature. One should
notice, too, that Shakespeare's appreciation of plenitude never
implies the denial of other values. The critical glance at
virginity referred to earlier is not single in its intent. Theseus
is asking Hermia to consider the advantages of two ways of

---

[15] Plato, *The Symposium*, Jowett's translation.
[16] "Substance" here does not of course mean "matter." It means that
which constitutes the thing itself, as in *Richard II*, 4.1.299, where the
substance of the grief lies in the soul.

life—the way of the convent and the way of marriage. It is the eve of his wedding, and there is no doubt of his bias. Still—

> Therefore, fair Hermia, question your desires,
> Know of your youth, examine well your blood,
> Whether, if you yield not to your father's choice,
> You can endure the livery of a nun,
> For aye to be in shady cloister mew'd,
> To live a barren sister all your life,
> Chanting faint hymns to the cold fruitless moon.
> Thrice blessed they that master so their blood
> To undergo such maiden pilgrimage,
> But earthlier happy is the rose distill'd,
> Than that which withering on the virgin thorn
> Grows, lives, and dies in single blessedness.[17]

To the holy life there is, after all, a triple blessedness; and the happy wife is only "earthlier" happy. One gathers that with Shakespeare the blessedness and the happiness were not equal, but it is clear that his preference for one does not blind him to the values of the other.

Further on in her conversation with Socrates, Diotima speaks of the relation between the desire for immortality and the love of fame. Her association of them is naturally more reasoned than Shakespeare's, though his is just as actual. But it is not quite accurate to say that he associated them. It is we who have disassociated the aspects of creation. But to return to Diotima! "Do you imagine," she asked, "that Alcestis would have died to save Admetus, or Achilles to avenge Patroclus . . . if they had not imagined that the memory of their virtues, which still survive them, would be immortal? Nay . . . I am persuaded that all men do all things, and the better they are the more they do them, in the hope of the glorious fame of immortal virtue. . . ." Later Shakespeare was to come to something like this himself. From the be-

[17] *A Midsummer Night's Dream*, 1.1.67-78.

ginning he had assumed the high worth of reputation, and by the time he was writing the great tragedies the most meaningful aspect of fame was for him the reputation for virtue—the hope of the tragic heroes that the memory of their virtues would survive them. At the close of the play, Othello, recognizing his error and resolving to make such amends as he can, finds that his services to the state and the bravery and justice of what he is about to do are the greatest reality. He asks that his acts be reported without apology or malice so that his good name, restored, may live behind him. At the close of his play Hamlet asks Horatio to live and tell his story, lest to future times he bear a "wounded name." Each of them has at last struggled through to a victory over an opposing force which had been in part within him. Flights of angels sing Hamlet to his rest, while Othello's soul is to be washed "in steep-down gulfs of liquid fire"; but the earthly reward of each is good name. Shakespeare's earlier concern had been to replace the old worn-out mortality with a new and similar existence and with the immortality of poetry. In some of the later sonnets mortality is found to be tainted with something more ghastly than transience. In this view the power of "sinful earth" to recreate itself does not console, and at the close of the sonnets the body is rejected that the soul may live. Later, in the great tragedies, the love of earth and the horror of mortality stand side by side, and neither diminishes the other. Lear at the height of his madness rejects the body, but he asks immediately to have his imagination sweetened; and the imaginative power in which Shakespeare's final plays are conceived *is* sweetened, as in the hymn at the betrothal of Ferdinand and Miranda,

> Honour, riches, marriage blessing,
> Long continuance and increasing. . . .
> Spring come to you at the farthest
> In the very end of harvest!

The Young Man's Beauty

THE sonnets which Shakespeare addressed to the young man were apparently written over a period of four or five years. At least the story they glance at covers some such time, for a sonnet[1] which does not belong with either the first or the last celebrates the third anniversary of the friendship. The precise duration of the story is neither demonstrable nor, for the purposes of this study, important. One need only think of it as occupying enough time for the development of the shifts in attitude which it discloses. In the later poems the poet's attitude toward the young man is a very different matter from the almost unqualified admiration of the opening sequence. There one reads of his beauty, his sweetness, his obstinate bachelorhood which forbids the immortality which children can bestow, and of the poet's resolution to immortalize the young man in poetry. For all their excellence, none of these seventeen sonnets is one of Shakespeare's best. However, the sequence is immediately followed by a sonnet which has become the possession of all English-speaking peoples. Although the primary purpose of the poem is to promise the friend an immortality in verse, it has won its fame through the sweetness with which the poet employs natural imagery to convey his early impressions of the young man.

"Sweet" and "sweetness" are nowadays terms of derogation, used only in the sense of "sugared" or "sugary." The older senses of the word—"fresh," "unspoiled," and "unseasoned"—are now restricted to the kitchen, as in "sweet cream" and "sweet [that is, unsalted] butter." "The sweet young thing" of not so long ago has disappeared as a type, and it would be quite rude to use the phrase for the few sports, biologically speaking, which now and then crop up. But it was different with Shakespeare. "Sweet" was his favorite epithet, and it is easy to see why. It describes a quality he admired and a state which recurs in his verse from the beginning to the end of his career. It is a quality which the early sonnets admire in the young man, and it is the quality of the opening lines of the eighteenth sonnet:

> Shall I compare thee to a summer's day?
> Thou art more lovely and more temperate:
> Rough winds do shake the darling buds of May . . .

This is the aspect of Shakespeare's writing which, considered alone, has won him the reputation for unconscious artistry. It is assumed that no poet would have made so ready a comparison in such commonplace terms ("summer's day," "lovely," and "darling") if he had had his craftsman's wits about him. Still less would he have been completely successful. Simple and natural it is, but it is only the beginning of the poem. The next line employs legal terminology with reference to nature, a usage which must have been startling at the time the poem was written:

> And summer's lease hath all too short a date.

He continues with a quatrain of notable artistry:

> Sometime too hot the eye of heaven shines,
> And often is his gold complexion dimm'd;
> And every fair from fair sometime declines,
> By chance or nature's changing course untrimm'd . . .

He then returns to the opening image in verse of comparable simplicity but fuller tone and deeper feeling, and concludes with a promise of immortality which, for the first time in the sonnets, is fully realized:

> But thy eternal summer shall not fade,
> Nor lose possession of that fair thou ow'st;
> Nor shall death brag thou wander'st in his shade,
> When in eternal lines to time thou grow'st:

> So long as men can breathe, or eyes can see,
> So long lives this, and this gives life to thee.

It is a poem celebrating three things: the poet's power, the young man's beauty, and his unspoiled nature. Although it is not one of Shakespeare's greatest poems, it approaches perfection. The thing to be noticed is the sonnet's skillful and varied presentation of its subject matter; and we should notice in passing that with the poet's celebration of his friend there is the concomitant disclosure of himself. The more one studies the sonnets in search of the young man, the more one learns of Shakespeare.

The qualities of the young friend which the opening sonnets insist upon are his beauty and temperateness. The temperateness was soon to change, but the beauty remained to the end. It is surely only a captious reader who will suppose that the "wrinkles" referred to in the seventy-seventh sonnet are anything more than such signs of maturity as a man in his early twenties may wear, for the reference is found in a quatrain insisting on the almost imperceptible advance of time—"the dial's shady stealth," "time's thievish progress to eternity." Still, the wrinkles have won their celebrants among Shakespeare's critics. A sentence of Dr. Johnson's will be sufficient answer: "Why sir, we must allow for some exaggeration." Once in the sonnets[2] Shakespeare described himself as "beated and chopp'd with tann'd antiquity," although he does not even look that old in the Droeshout portrait. Deeply aware of mutability, he knew intellectually that there must be a change in the friend, though he could not see it:

> Ah, yet doth beauty, like a dial hand,
> Steal from his figure, and no pace perceiv'd;
> So your sweet hue, which methinks still doth stand,
> Hath motion, and mine eye may be deceiv'd. . . .[3]

[2] Sonnet 62. [3] Sonnet 104.

Physically the young man is represented as the embodiment of nature's best, excelling all contemporary excellence and recalling only the departed glories of the past. "All this," as Shakespeare remarked in another connection, "the world well knows."

What is not so often noticed is that from the very beginning the poet is concerned with more than the physical, and that the concern increases as the poems proceed. There is a growing emphasis on what it was once common to call "moral beauty." That we no longer do so is, I take it, another instance of our tendency to dissociate matters formerly thought related. It is not that as Shakespeare progressed he abandoned his concern with physical beauty, but rather that beauty was not taken to be exclusively physical. And it is abundantly demonstrated that Shakespeare did not take inward and outward beauty to be identical. Although it was fashionable in his time to talk about the coincidence of inward and outward beauty, to believe that the physically beautiful must be good, Shakespeare never took the notion seriously. It bubbles to the surface of the dialogue now and then. In *The Tempest* it helps to characterize Shakespeare's most innocent heroine, who exclaims, on first seeing Ferdinand, that "nothing ill can dwell in such a temple." But the idea had been demonstrably false since the time of Helen of Troy, and Shakespeare was much too sensible to do more than toy with it. On the desperate morning after her violation the notion occurred to Lucrece, but she recalled the disparity between Tarquin's appearance and his heart and quickly rejected it. Shakespeare's characteristic insistence is upon the difference between appearance and reality, between the realms of the eye and the mind, the eye and the heart.

It is equally characteristic of him to find that the discrepancy between appearance and reality is the more horrible in proportion as the appearance promises values the reality does not disclose. He assumed that one could expect much from a young man as handsomely endowed as his friend. So it happened that as qualities which Shakespeare did not admire emerged with the young man's maturing, the poet's admiration became qualified—in different ways and for different reasons, but always reluctantly. He seems to have been the sort of person who wanted to think well of those he liked, and whenever possible to return to a good opinion formerly held. In the middle sonnets the young man is praised for mildness and temperance without, it appears, always good reason. The poet's responses to change in the young friend are varied, but perhaps if we look closely at them they will conform to some sort of pattern.

From the poet's point of view the youth's affair with the dark lady was clearly an instance of both inconstancy and intemperance, yet it seems to have mattered less than other things. The greatest threats to the friendship were offences of the spirit. I trust that no one will suppose me to assert that an illicit affair, adulterous on the woman's part, is by its nature purely a physical matter. It is simply that Shakespeare at first viewed it, or chose to view it, as of relatively minor importance to him. It is often said that Shakespeare introduced the young woman to his friend, who seduced her. This interpretation is a credit to our chivalry and does little harm as long as we remember that it is a way of speaking, but it does not represent the situation depicted in the sonnets and seems to have little to do with the view of life presented in the plays. In all of Shakespeare's plays the virtuous woman is very little endangered and, by standards of later literature, very little restrained. She normally does the proposing, especially if she finds the lover's reticence to be motivated by some circumstance of honor or a condition considerable only to the male mind. Desdemona gave Othello the "hint" on which he spoke, and on the night of their first meeting Juliet leaned over the balcony and said to Romeo,

Three words, dear Romeo, and good night indeed.
If that thy bent of love be honourable,
Thy purpose marriage, send me word to-morrow. . . .

The dark lady is presented as already married and altogether unrestrained. She wooed the young man and won him. Shakespeare found the situation difficult but not surprising:

Gentle thou art, and therefore to be won,
Beauteous thou art, therefore to be assail'd;
And when a woman woos, what woman's son
Will sourly leave her till she have prevail'd?[4]

The willing seduction of the youth is looked upon as the inevitable consequence of her attractive wantonness and of his youth and beauty. The "truth" that is broken is the woman's to the poet, and what is threatened is the friendship between the two men. It is the latter which troubles Shakespeare the more, as the forty-second sonnet discloses:

That thou hast her, it is not all my grief,
And yet it may be said I lov'd her dearly;
That she hath thee is of my wailing chief,
A loss in love that touches me more nearly. . . .

The attitude disclosed by these lines is consistent with Shakespeare's overall treatment of friendship and the sins of the flesh. He sometimes regards sexual indulgence as an evil excess of something which is good in itself. He is most stern with libertinism in which habit has worn away the sense of transgression, or in which there is no indication that it ever existed—Lucio in *Measure for Measure*, Paris and Helen, and, in the sonnets, the dark lady. He is not very tolerant of sexual freedom erected into a principle, nor is he generally cordial to unprincipled transgressors, unless they are people of whom not much could be expected, and such characters— Doll Tearsheet, for example—are at last overtaken by their

[4] Sonnet 41.

past. In the sixty-sixth sonnet's list of disheartening things he places "maiden virtue rudely strumpeted." We should notice that it is not the loss of virginity. Soiled virtue, he keeps saying, may reassert itself, may, through experience, become stronger than before. The line refers to the destruction not of virginity but of virtue. His attitude is not that our acts do not matter or that we can escape their consequences (he is, of course, too honest an observer to be diagrammatic in his recreations of life) but that all commissions of the same act are not equally culpable. His greatest sympathy is for the intelligent man who cannot in spite of himself "Shun the heaven that leads men to this hell." The most striking instance of this is Antony.

Students of Shakespeare are so heavily indebted to Professor Harbage that it is possible to differ with him only after long consideration. In one of his books[5] he takes the view that Shakespeare loved the sinner while hating the sin. "What Shakespeare does is to remove the onus from agents and place it on the thing itself: he does not punish evil persons and reward virtuous ones, but condemns evil and praises virtue by portraying their contrasted effects." This is nicely put. It is, in fact, almost as one could wish it. It notices Shakespeare's almost constant refusal to divide his characters into good and evil persons, and it recognizes the complexity of the dramatist's judgment which enables even a villain's virtues to shine by their own light. But surely Professor Harbage's dissociation of evil and the evildoer makes Shakespeare's art more abstract than it is. Is it not too simple an accounting for the indulgence often shown the characters? Later he quotes Hamlet on Claudius:

> Bloody, bawdy villain!
> Remorseless, treacherous, lecherous, kindless villain!

[5] Alfred Harbage, *As They Liked It*, The Macmillan Company, New York, 1947, p. 123.

And he observes that murder is viewed with loathing because it is "kindless."[6] "The most highly valued quality of kindness, humanity, the 'virtue of compassion,' finds its opposite essence in the spirit of the murderer. . . ." It is just so. There is always Shakespeare's detestation of inhumanity. And might it not also be that the commission of a sin is sometimes viewed with tolerance because it *is* human? And could it be considered so apart from the agent? Is not the difference between the transgressions of Claudio and Lucio in *Measure for Measure* pretty much the essence of each agent and not the act itself? Can there be many instances in which it is possible to weigh the act apart from the agent? Lucio's acts are the deliberate procurement of pleasure at whatever cost to his partner; Claudio's transgression is the almost spontaneous overflow of honest passion. It is possible to argue that right is right and wrong is wrong, and that there can be no mitigating circumstances; but if this were the view of all dramatic writers there would be nothing but melodrama and morality plays. The interesting and finally dramatic thing is the relation of the man to the act. This could be abundantly illustrated in the plays; the sonnets are too barren of events to permit discussion of the matter in connection with the young man. However, the attitude toward the young man, and the assumptions on which the attitude rests, are of a piece with the plays. The young and handsome friend, tempted, is less culpable than the temptress, less culpable than the poet in his relations with her, for the poet was older and, like the woman, bound by vows of truth. On the young man's part the connection was not adulterous, but the difference in the depicted guilt of each party is not simply the difference between adultery and fornication. Shakespeare

---

[6] *Ibid.*, p. 182. Perhaps a more primary meaning of *kindless* is *nature-less, unnatural*, and, more specifically in the context, *incestuous*. On the other hand no one would want to question the general meaning of Professor Harbage's sentence.

does not view behavior in so abstract a way. Categories of behavior, no matter how necessary to the institutionalization of ethics, were not often adequate to his exposition of specific instances. The poet's tendency was to forgive the young man's sexual transgression to a degree to which he did not forgive himself or the dark lady, and to which he did not forgive the young man in other matters.

Much has been written on Shakespeare's admiration for the young man and the indulgence he showed him. Very little has been written on the critical aspects of the poet's attitude toward him. Let us turn to that. The reproaches to the youth are sometimes tentative, sometimes, in the way of friendship, softened with compliments. In the forty-first sonnet the young man's wrongs are "petty wrongs." He is told[7] that he is justly praised, but that, "being fond on praise" (that is, fond of praise), he reduces the value of it, and that the world which praises his "outward" (that is, his physical appearance and bearing) can see the beauty of his mind only in his deeds. He is warned that his misdeeds are not unnoticed, that men look at his appearance, "thy fair flower," and "add the rank smell of weeds."[8]

> But why thy odour matcheth not thy show,
> The soil is this, that thou dost common grow.

He is reminded that when inner reality does not square with appearance, beauty is like Eve's apple,[9] and that although for the moment he lends a kind of beauty to his vices, good reputation will in time be destroyed by unworthy acts.[10] These attempts at paraphrase in the interest of brevity are necessarily inadequate; a paraphrase of poetic irony would be worse than useless. Some of the ironical reproaches are:

> Farewell, thou art too dear for my possessing,
> And like enough thou know'st thy estimate. . . .[11]

[7] Sonnet 84.　　[8] Sonnet 69.　　[9] Sonnet 93.
[10] Sonnet 95.　　[11] Sonnet 87.

> When love, converted from the thing it was,
> Shall reasons find of settled gravity. . . .[12]

> I found, or thought I found, you did exceed
> The barren tender of a poet's debt. . . .[13]

There is no need to exhaust the store of reproaches, and it would be idle to try to indicate most of the occasions which called them forth. Many of the reproaches, such as the one on his growing common, could have been provoked by a number of actions. The only ones with a knowable basis are those arising from the affair with the dark lady. Other references to offenses of a like sort may possibly glance at other women, as in,

> How many lambs might the stern wolf betray,
> If like a lamb he could his looks translate!
> How many gazers mightst thou lead away,
> If thou wouldst use the strength of all thy state.[14]

There are other reproaches for which the cause cannot even be guessed, the poems disclosing no more than that the young man had not fulfilled his promise.

The reproaches to which Shakespeare attached the greatest importance are, although abstracted from events, clear enough. They hint at a certain arrogance in the young man and tell of his growing self-importance, a fault which at one time threatened the existence of the friendship. In one of the sonnets Shakespeare suggested that perhaps the friend might have given his friendship before he knew his own worth, or that he had mistaken Shakespeare's. In any case, mutuality destroyed, the young man's gift of friendship is returned to him:

> Farewell, thou art too dear for my possessing,
> And like enough thou know'st thy estimate:
> The charter of thy worth gives thee releasing;

[12] Sonnet 49.   [13] Sonnet 83.   [14] Sonnet 96.

My bonds in thee are all determinate.
For how do I hold thee but by thy granting?
And for that riches where is my deserving?
The cause of this fair gift in me is wanting,
And so my patent back again is swerving.
Thyself thou gav'st, thy own worth then not knowing,
Or me, to whom thou gav'st it else mistaking;
So thy great gift, upon misprision growing,
Comes home again, on better judgment making.
  Thus have I had thee, as a dream doth flatter,
  In sleep a king, but waking no such matter.[15]

Throughout the poem the genuine regret is stated with gentle
irony. The reader is always aware of the poet's belief in his
own worth. In other sonnets the poet's worthiness is insisted
upon. Although he realizes that he has not done all he could
to keep the friendship in repair, his protestations of the constancy and disinterestedness of his affection have the stamp
of truth. It might appear, he seems to say, that I cultivate
your friendship for prudential reasons, but it is not so. There
are those who glory in birth, skill, wealth, strength, possessions, and outward show, but "these particulars are not
my measure,"

  Thy love is better than high birth to me,
  Richer than wealth, prouder than garments' cost. . . .[16]

And this, too, is consistent with the point of view disclosed
by the works as a whole.

Shakespeare nowhere either says or implies that birth and
wealth are unimportant. Quite the contrary! They are admired for certain values, but they are never admired for themselves alone. His is a world in which all things have their
uses and do not readily divide themselves into the sacred and
the profane. It is apparent that he places a high value on
beauty, birth, wealth, and wit, but he insists that though the

[15] Sonnet 87.   [16] Sonnet 91.

friend might have "any of these all, or all, or more,"[17] his friendship is "engrafted to" the young man's truth and worth. "Builded far from accident,"

> It suffers not in smiling pomp, nor falls
> Under the blow of thralled discontent. . . .[18]

It is an attitude consistent with his awareness of the transient glory of "great princes' favorites"[19] and his insistence on the prior value of the things of the mind and spirit. In sonnet number one hundred twenty-five he dissociates himself from the "dwellers on form and favor," the "pitiful thrivers" who "lose all and more by paying too much rent."

This is a point of view often forgotten by those who attempt to base their concept of Shakespeare on the external records of his career, which show quite plainly that he was a good businessman. But we ought to remember that the records are only a partial disclosure of the man. His plays, which also show a respect for wealth and position, do not regard them, as we have said, as ends in themselves, and in the sonnets he never accords them a primary value. There are two plays which deal specifically with riches, *The Merchant of Venice* and *Timon of Athens*, and, as G. Wilson Knight has pointed out,[20] "in both they are contrasted with a greater value." Although Portia is an heiress and Bassanio the more attracted to her because of her riches, only an easy cynicism could deny their love or suppose that Bassanio's story is that of a young man who did well; and Timon treasures more highly than riches "the richer values in himself." I do not want to say much of *Timon*. It is an unfinished work, and its thematic pattern is therefore incomplete. One cannot tell to what extent the dramatist's thought would have been qualified by juxtapositions which he intended

---

[17] Sonnet 37.   [18] Sonnet 124.   [19] Sonnet 25.
[20] G. Wilson Knight, *The Olive and the Sword*, Oxford University Press, 1944, pp. 89-90.

and never made. Still, Knight's point is beyond question. There is also a certain parallel between Timon and the poet of the sonnets: there is the appreciation of wealth and the subordination of it to other values, chiefly friendship, and there is the recognition of "richer values in himself." It is so throughout Shakespeare, and it is not easy to see how some critics came to wish it otherwise. Every sensible person will regard economic security and the respect of his fellow men as good things, and he will be pleased at Shakespeare's failure to sentimentalize poverty and low birth. Perhaps at first he will be troubled a bit by Shakespeare's insistence on his own worthiness, but further study should put him at ease. Let us look for a moment at the many-sidedness of Shakespeare's self-view.

"The web of life is of a mingled yarn, good and ill together," remarks a character in *All's Well*, who then continues, "our virtues would be proud if our faults whipped them not. . . ." It was Shakespeare's way to be aware of his virtues and to whip them with his faults. Further, he was constantly aware, as we shall see later, of the faults of virtue. So it happens that in the self-view which the sonnets present, there is self-knowledge without self-satisfaction. He proclaims his worth as a poet in many sonnets, and quite as often he acknowledges his faults. On both scores he was quite right. The contempt he expresses for the rival poet is saved from arrogance by his admiration for the rival's technical excellence. He asserts the worth of the friendship with the young man while fearing its dissolution. The fear has many sources: that "thou may'st take all this away," that "the filching age will steal his treasure,"[21] and his own actions. He confesses that, full of the friend's "ne'er-cloying sweetness," he turned to "bitter sauces,"[22] as a healthy person turns to medicine to prevent sickness. There is a good deal

[21] Sonnet 75.   [22] Sonnet 118.

in this "bitter sauces" vein, and it looks at first like rationalization. It may be that it is. The point here is the existence of self-admitted follies. The most revealing thing about the apprehensions is the regret which almost always accompanies or follows them. There are times when he regards his apprehensions as a kind of—could we say?—hypochondria of the spirit, and he apologizes for it, recognizing it as a sin against friendship, which, Ellen Terry supposed,[23] was to him "the most sacred of all human relations."

It was Shakespeare's way, and it increased as he matured, to notice the obverse sides of things, of even his own devotion, as later instances will show. He is, of course, saved from inaction by his gusto and his conviction. I should not like to suggest a considerable alloy of Prufrock in him. For the moment we are taking his vigor for granted while we point out that action, while never evaded, is not always clear. His self-awareness, like his outward view, is always multiple. While he protests that his own friendship is "not mix'd with seconds" and "knows no art,"[24] he is not always sure that the friend can meet him on terms of a personal equality transcending all other considerations; in short, he is not always certain that his friendship is returned in kind. In the twenty-third sonnet, his first apology for neglecting the friend, he gives as the reason for his silence "fear of trust." There is the recurrent fear that the love given openly is not fully returned[25] and might be misconstrued.

In the plays the most admirable characters are those who give themselves without reservation, and often the most poignant passages are those in which the freely given affection is betrayed. Hamlet is the world's best-loved tragic hero because in a sense he wears his heart upon his sleeve. He had idealized his mother, set his heart upon Ophelia, and

---

[23] Ellen Terry, *Four Lectures on Shakespeare*. Martin Hopkinson Ltd., 23 Soho Square, London, 1932, p. 177.
[24] Sonnet 125.   [25] See Sonnet 61.

made friends with Rosencranz and Guildenstern. Their betrayal of Hamlet's trust is one of the chief motives of the action of the play. Nor is his lovableness reduced by his recurrent savagery, which, in one way or another, is motivated by his devotion. He was cruel to his mother "only to be kind," and since he knew nothing more contemptible than a friendship based on policy, he sent his college friends to their deaths: "Why man, they did make love to this employment." Nor could Othello's tragedy have developed without the wholeness of his love. There is not a character giving his heart wholly—and it does not matter how imprudent the giving may be—who does not in a large measure win Shakespeare's admiration. Wholeheartedness is not only for Shakespeare's lovers; it is for husband and wife, father and daughter, mother and son, brothers, sisters, friends. It is what he feared from the beginning the young man might not be capable of.

Even in the sonnets of the opening sequence, the most adulatory of all, it occurred to him that perhaps the young man remained single because he had "no love toward others."[26] There is the clear parallel to Narcissus, the perfectly beautiful youth who disdained the nymphs because he loved himself. In the tenth sonnet Shakespeare notes that although the young man inspires love in others he does not return it. To be sure, the opening sonnets treat largely of the love for woman, or rather the lack of it, but the suspected coldness is not sexual; it is of the heart. Should it turn out that the suspicion is justified, it would represent to the poet an insuperable obstacle to the friendship.

With Shakespeare the essence of friendship, as of love, is mutuality; and in the sonnets there is the recurrent fear that the basis of moral equality which mutuality demands does not exist. In one of his greatest sonnets[27] the ideal friendship

[26] Sonnet 9.　　　　　　　　　　　　[27] Sonnet 116.

is described as "the marriage of true minds," a state which he refuses to consider unattainable:

> Let me not to the marriage of true minds
> Admit impediments.

Friendship is not true friendship which wavers because of a change in one of the friends, or which succumbs to the machinations of an outsider:

> Love is not love
> Which alters when it alteration finds,
> Or bends with the remover to remove.

Its worth, like that of the star by which the mariner steers his course, is beyond estimation; yet like the mariner who knows the star is fixed in its place, we know the friendship, being true, is fixed, and that we can guide our course by it:

> . . . it is an ever-fixed mark,
> That looks on tempests and is never shaken;
> It is the star to every wandering bark,
> Whose worth's unknown, although his height be taken.

It does not, like physical beauty, fade with time. If this is not true, there is no truth, no reality, Shakespeare himself has never written, and no man has ever loved. This is his standard of friendship. He hopes to be equal to it. Could the friend attain it? Not, it would appear, if the reproach made tentatively in the early sonnets should, after all, turn out to have been justified:

> For shame, deny that thou bear'st love to any,
> Who for thyself art so unprovident.
> Grant, if thou wilt, thou art belov'd of many,
> But that thou none lov'st is most evident.[28]

Shakespeare came in time to fear that his friend's estimate of him would have a prudential basis, and that, the friend-

[28] Sonnet 10.

ship failing, the friend would reject him and rationalize the rejection:

> Against that time, if ever that time come,
> When I shall see thee frown on my defects,
> When as thy love has cast his utmost sum,
> Call'd to that audit by advis'd respects;
> Against that time when thou shalt strangely pass,
> And scarcely greet me with that sun, thine eye,
> When love, converted from the thing it was,
> Shall reasons find of settled gravity. . . .[29]

In the sonnets the assumption of the need for mutuality (it is this assumption which justifies the identity metaphor) is strong enough to motivate the further assumption that when mutuality is known not to exist, the end is in sight and might better be anticipated:

> Then hate me when thou wilt; if ever, now;
> Now while the world is bent my deeds to cross,
> Join with the spite of fortune, make me bow,
> And do not drop in for an afterloss:
> Ah, do not, when my heart hath 'scap'd this sorrow,
> Come in the rearward of a conquer'd woe;
> Give not a windy night a rainy morrow,
> To linger out a purpos'd overthrow. . . .[30]

The sonnets to the young man begin with celebrations of his beauty, but they move in time to realms in which physical beauty is overshadowed by things of greater importance, the young friend's integrity, for instance, and his capacity for mature and responsible relationships with his fellow men. These are the matters which come to be insisted upon. The sonnets declare that if the promise shown by the young man early in the sonnets is not fulfilled, his outward appearance is of little worth.

[29] Sonnet 49. [30] Sonnet 90.

The Economy of the Closed Heart

THERE is no idea to which Shakespeare returns more often than the doctrine taught by the parable of the talents. It is referred to and expounded at length in the dialogue of the plays. It is often a major dramatic theme. In the sonnets it is no less prominent than in the plays. In both it is glanced at on innumerable occasions, when, most often, it is taken as correlative to an idea of more immediate importance. None of Shakespeare's ideas is more fixed or serves more often as a measure of character. The idea is, of course, the concept of man's stewardship referred to in the discussion of plenitude. Shakespeare's use of it in connection with propagation will indicate to modern readers the pervasiveness of his belief in it. In the very first sonnet the young man was told that he consumed himself in not giving himself, and in the fourth he was warned that "Nature's bequest gives nothing, but doth lend." The point invariably made is that we hold our possessions in trust, that we are the stewards and not the owners of our excellence. It is our function to employ our excellence to the best of our ability. Conversely, the man who simply preserves what he is entrusted with is regarded as the "wicked and slothful servant" of the parable, who said "I was afraid, and went, and hid thy talent in the earth: lo, there thou hast that is thine." Shakespeare states his view of the matter at the opening of *Measure for Measure*:

> Thyself and thy belongings
> Are not thine own so proper, as to waste
> Thyself upon thy virtues, they on thee.
> Heaven doth with us as we with torches do,
> Not light them for themselves; for if our virtues
> Did not go forth of us, 'twere all alike
> As if we had them not. Spirits are not finely touch'd
> But to fine issues, nor Nature never lends

> The smallest scruple of her excellence,
> But, like a thrifty goddess, she determines
> Herself the glory of a creditor,
> Both thanks and use.[1]

In this instance the idea is allied to another of his most pervasive convictions—the belief that a virtue cannot finally be said to exist until it has expressed itself in action. Of that, more later. These ideas are among the *données* of Shakespeare's thought. When they are not made explicit, their values are always assumed.

Here I should like to consider two of Shakespeare's most disputed sonnets in connection with this aspect of his thought. I do not suppose that what is said will exhaust the poems, yet we may hope to arrive at a basic understanding of them and a nearer view of the young man to whom they were addressed. The last chapter noticed Shakespeare's distrust of a certain cool prudence in the friend, the quality standing in contrast to the openness of heart to which he was himself committed. It is in connection with this prudence that Shakespeare later referred to the friend as one of those who are "the lords and owners of their faces," and it allies him with the servant who hid his talent in the earth. One of the most disputed lines in the sonnets—"A man in hue, all hues in his controlling"—will make a kind of good sense if we turn to it with Shakespeare's ideas on man's stewardship in mind. Since the poet's complexity was never more teasingly expressed, it will be well to quote the entire poem:

> A woman's face with Nature's own hand painted
> Hast thou, the master-mistress of my passion:
> A woman's gentle heart, but not acquainted
> With shifting change, as is false women's fashion;
> An eye more bright than theirs, less false in rolling,
> Gilding the object whereupon it gazeth;

[1] 1.1.30-41.

A man in hue, all hues in his controlling,
Which steals men's eyes and women's souls amazeth.
And for a woman wert thou first created;
Till Nature, as she wrought thee, fell a-doting,
And by addition me of thee defeated,
By adding one thing to my purpose nothing.
    But since she prick'd thee out for women's pleasure,
    Mine be thy love, and thy love's use their treasure.[2]

It seems to say, "You have, my friend, the beauty of a woman and so many feminine qualities that you command the attention of men and amaze women. Indeed it seems that nature first intended you for a woman, but as she created you she absent-mindedly gave you male genitals and thus removed you from the realm of man's desire. Your friendship is therefore mine, but your 'love's use' is woman's."

Though primarily a playful poem, it is far from simple. The off-color jest of the closing lines has troubled many readers, and the second line has aroused much controversy. Steevens, in 1780, found it "impossible to read this fulsome panegyrick, addressed to a male object, without an equal mixture of disgust and indignation."[3] His passion is ill-spent, yet the odd masculine assumption that masculinity is best expressed by indignation is a common one. The phrase "master-mistress" has been the undoing both of those critics who feared a homosexual interpretation and of those eager for it. A less passionate view might be more productive. The basic attitude of the poem, the wit aside, is that of Tennyson for Hallam, whose "manhood fused with female grace" so captivated him. Tennyson could write,

> But thou that fillest all the room
> Of all my love. . . .

[2] Sonnet 20.
[3] See "The Variorum Shakespeare," *The Sonnets*, ed. Hyder E. Rollins, J. B. Lippincott Company, Philadelphia and London, 1944, for this and other comments.

though there was, of course, Emily. It is a poet's way of speaking about an emotional reality. It would not be to the point to object that in writing as he did Tennyson was under the influence of Shakespeare's sonnets. Of course he was, but he was using the sonnets to find his way to his own feelings.

In a Freudian sense the feelings of both poets *were* sexual; it is a matter of definition. I do not mean that either was homosexual, and I will have no truck with the facile psychologizing which makes it possible to say that a man was homosexual although neither he nor any of his acquaintances knew it. That would be to discount Shakespeare's capacity for perception in favor of our own. Shakespeare was well aware of his emotion for the young man, just as he was aware that the realm of the emotions is a continuum of which sexual emotion is a part. He could recognize areas in the realm of the affections without categorizing them. He understood the uses of the categories which man imposes on the realm of nature in his attempt to understand it, but he did not confuse the categories with the things on which they are imposed. He knew that clear divisions occur only in the categories. The Freudians use the word "sexuality" to denote *all the impulses* which draw human beings together. It is only in this sense that the emotion of Shakespeare and Tennyson could be called sexual. The point is that Shakespeare, like Freud, recognized the continuity of the emotions. With Shakespeare affection is a universal, and his name for it is love.

Perhaps it will not falsify the matter to put it this way: The affection felt for a member of one's own sex is identical with the affection felt for a member of the opposite sex, although to this latter sexual attraction may be added. The affection itself is neither male nor female; it is one. Shakespeare, then, like modern psychology, assumes the universality of affection, and in this sonnet he remarks that his affection for the young man might under other circumstances —that is, had the young man been a woman—have taken a sexual turn. The awareness of the nature of affection is strong enough to suggest the fantasy of the friend's creation —"Nature, as she wrought thee, fell a-doting"—and all that modern psychology tells us assures us that it is not "abnormal." It is simply that Shakespeare called things by their best names. From this point of view it is natural for a man to speak of his "love" for any human being, a woman, child, or another man. Indeed it is still fairly common for educated people to use the word in this way, though the usage is spurned by those who are merely sophisticated.

The sonnet under discussion is not an important poem. The rimes are too ingenious, and its parts seem almost designed to distract the reader from the poem as a whole. I say "seem" because I imagine that it is only later generations who have found this difficulty, and that to Shakespeare's contemporaries the poem was far from troublesome. Taken on Shakespeare's terms, the poem achieves a modest success. If we accept the ambivalence of the friend's attractiveness, we need not be troubled by the nice balancing of qualities—a woman's face and heart (the poem was apparently written early in the friendship) and not so much a more than feminine constancy as a less than feminine fickleness. His eye, brighter than woman's, bestows a luster upon all the objects of its gaze. He is a man of such qualities that all qualities in others are placed under his control. Critics have found "hue" to be enigmatic, and it may well be that the first readers of the sonnets saw in it a reference now lost to us; but although a knowledge of the reference would give us valuable historical or biographical data, it is not needed for a basic comprehension of the poem. "Hue" means "complexion," and "in hue" means the state in which the humors are properly mixed. Since the young man is not dominated by any one passion, his passions are in the control of his reason. In Shakespeare's characteristic view this state of affairs is admirable almost to the point of inhumanity. The primary purpose of the line is to indicate the young man's power to dominate, perhaps without conscious intent and clearly without the assumption of responsibility. This power, the poem suggests, is a feminine attribute. The regard of the poet for the young man is so clearly conveyed in this sonnet that the implied, gentle, and laughing criticism has passed unnoticed. A full view of the poem will not find that it is flattering in all its aspects, nor was it intended to be.

In our time there was once a youth of one-and-twenty whose approach to emotion was simpler than Shakespeare's. He listened to his elders, and in due time he found that his experience squared with what he had been told. One day he had heard a wise man say that

> "The heart out of the bosom
> Was never given in vain;
> 'Tis paid with sighs a plenty
> And sold for endless rue."
>
> And I am two-and-twenty,
> And oh, 'tis true, 'tis true.[4]

In this poem the hurt of the open heart is observed in isolation and with a sentimentality nicely appropriate to twenty-two. Or perhaps the pain had not been isolated; it may be that it had subsumed all the other aspects of the experience. In either case it is what a well-lettered young man of melancholy spirit is supposed to feel, and it is what this particular young man had been taught to feel. It will serve as a contrast to Shakespeare's way of apprehending the same thing. In the Housman poem the view of the situation is simplicity itself: the heart gives itself in vain. It does not heed the wise men, and it learns that they were right. If we were to go

[4] "When I was one-and-twenty" in *A Shropshire Lad*.

beyond the poem, we could only suppose that the young man should have listened to his elders in the first place. In Shakespeare's view the open heart must give itself away in order to maintain its existence. It is confronted with a perpetual dilemma: it can know of its being only through self-loss. The alternative is to conserve itself until it has withered away. Both courses of action are illustrated in the plays; both are observed in the sonnets with an acuteness Shakespeare was never to exceed.

Shakespeare noticed the obverse sides of things. Although the sonnets proclaim his affection for the young man and his indulgence of him, they also disclose the attitudes which Shakespeare takes to both the affection and the indulgence. He forgives a trespass, and then, in the thirty-fifth sonnet, he apologizes for the presumption of forgiveness, for, in his words, "excusing thy sins more than thy sins are." We should notice that the forgiveness also involves a certain debasement on the poet's part: "Myself corrupting, salving thy amiss." Nor does he view simply his desire to change himself. In the one hundred and eleventh sonnet he regrets the fate which has made him a man of the theatre, which

> . . . did not better for my life provide
> Than public means which public manners breeds.

And although he assures the friend that he will do anything to wipe away this stain, he realizes that the cleansing in itself is a kind of stain. There would be a need for a "double penance"—to remove the stain and "to correct correction." Protesting on another occasion[5] that he does not care what the opinion of critic or flatterer may be, provided he has the good opinion of his friend, he comments, "In so profound abysm I throw all care." It is the recognition of the obverse of one of his most firmly held tenets. The recognition does not destroy the belief; there is, as with Hamlet, the coexistent

[5] Sonnet 112.

questioning of the value of the thing in which he believes. When the sonnets are aware that the friend's faults constitute a threat to the friendship, there is the recurrent accompaniment of ironic self-consciousness, arising, it appears, from a knowledge of the waywardness with which affection, in order to maintain its being in an imperfect world, bestows itself with imperfect cause. It must, at times, debase its currency in order to exist. The alternative to this dilemma is the economy of the closed heart.

The closed heart may be poor, but it is at ease. Those men are most content who, though they inspire affection in others, have no need of it themselves. They are the men "in hue, all hues in their controlling." They have the power to hurt, but they are not hurt. Their happiness is the ignorance of their incompleteness.

> They that have power to hurt and will do none,
> That do not do the thing they most do show,
> Who, moving others, are themselves as stone,
> Unmoved, cold, and to temptation slow;
> They rightly do inherit heaven's graces
> And husband nature's riches from expense;
> They are the lords and owners of their faces,
> Others but stewards of their excellence.
> The summer's flower is to the summer sweet,
> Though to itself it only live and die,
> But if that flower with base infection meet,
> The basest weed outbraves his dignity:
>   For sweetest things turn sourest by their deeds;
>   Lilies that fester smell far worse than weeds.[6]

Everything about the poem invites comment, from the private force of the opening phrases to the last line, which, one editor assures us, "is not true." The recorded conjectures about it are rich in everything that conjecture can lead to,

[6] Sonnet 94.

and in recent years it has been the object of more critical analyses than any other sonnet. If we approach it in the light of Shakespeare's other works, we might find it less difficult than it appears.

A survey of Shakespeare's works will show that this sonnet employs his most familiar imagery and that the thought of the sonnet, bit by bit, is to be found everywhere. Primarily it is the articulation of the parts which puzzles. On first reading the sonnet, we shall, of course, notice the irony of the first eight lines; and everything that we find in the other works will confirm it. It is preposterous on the face of things to proclaim as the inheritors of heaven's graces those who are "as stone." It can be other than ironical only to the cynic, for even the hardhearted man thinks of himself as generous and cherishes an abstract admiration for warmth. In addition, it will be noticed that what Shakespeare says here contradicts everything that he has said elsewhere on the subject. The irony of the octave is Swiftian in both method and force. In specious terms the poet states as true that which he is well known to consider false: those men whose appearance does not square with reality, whose deeds do not fulfill their promise, who move others while remaining cold, are proclaimed the heirs to heaven's graces. They are the owners of themselves, whereas throughout Shakespeare's works self-possession in the sense of living without regard for others is intolerable.

After the stinging "Others but stewards of their excellence," there is a full stop, and the poet turns to one of his most familiar images, the flower which is still beautiful although it lives to itself alone. The analogy is obvious. In the opening sequence the flower had been the emblem of the young man "contracted to his own bright eyes." Throughout the sonnets the poet praises the flower for its beauty, which he insists is only one of its attributes, and, he also insists from time to time, not its supreme one. The beauty, he repeats, is made fairer by its odor, which in turn becomes the symbol of that which is usefully good, or of the essential nature of the flower, or of both. In some sonnets the odor, or essence, may be distilled into perfume, in which case its odor will live "pent in walls of glass" after the flower has died. In other instances the distillation of essence is a symbol of procreation. In still others the odor of the flower symbolizes moral good:

> But why thy odour matcheth not thy show,
> The soil is this, that thou dost common grow.[7]

And,

> O, how much more doth beauty beauteous seem
> By that sweet ornament which truth doth give!
> The rose looks fair, but fairer we it deem
> For that sweet odour which doth in it live. . . .[8]

In the sonnet under discussion, the flower living to itself, and having therefore failed to fulfill its function, is incomplete, though it still has physical beauty; but if it should meet with infection (that is, if the expression of its function should be perverted), its odor (that is, its essence, its soul, its human utility as expressed in the deeds of the young man and the perfume of the flower) becomes worse than that of weeds, worse, that is, than that from which nothing was expected.

"They that have power to hurt" is both a great poem and an imperfect one. There is neither weakness nor relaxation. It should be noticed that the failure is not, as is often the case, one of fitting the matter to the form. There is neither tacking on nor repetition of matter to fill out the prescribed length. It is rather that the unity is marred by a change in tone, though not in intensity, at the close of the octave, and that the cohesion of parts depends upon a context of ideas

[7] Sonnet 69.   [8] Sonnet 54.

which are not sufficiently explicit in the poem, though they ought to be familiar to all readers of Shakespeare.

I do not want to appear to consider the poem clearer than it is. The first line is tauntingly obscure, and an understanding of the poem cannot proceed without an interpretation of it. However, it seems reasonable to resolve the enigma of "power to hurt" by reference to what follows and to other works of Shakespeare. This I have tried to do. The meaning of "do none" is apparent if we take it to be clarified by expansion in line two. It was sometimes Shakespeare's hasty way to say a thing obscurely and then to clarify it by repetition, as in *King Lear*:

> *Regan*:   I have hope
> You less know how to value her desert
> Than she to scant her duty.
> *Lear*: Say, how is that?
> *Regan*: I cannot think my sister in the least
> would fail her obligation.[9]

We may take it that the meaning of "do none" is restated in the line that follows: "That do not do the thing they most do show." This is quite clear, and its meaning is made specific in the next line: "Who, moving others, are themselves as stone." The "power to hurt" is, then, the power to move others by imposing on their unreciprocated loyalty, and "do none" is the condition of not doing what the loyal friend, because of his loyalty, had taken for granted. When Emilia discovers the murder of Desdemona and is threatened by Othello, she replies,

> Thou hast not half the power to do me harm
> As I have to be hurt.[10]

Her power to be hurt resides, of course, in her loyalty to Desdemona. As for the "base infection," there is no know-

[9] 2.4.140-144.   [10] 5.2.162.

ing what it specifically was, or what it threatened to be, for it is referred to conditionally in the poem and may have been apprehended rather than actual. But it is clear from the importance attached to it that it refers to some offence of the spirit, a denial of something Shakespeare held essential to decent humanity. "Perhaps," Rebecca West speculates,[11] "the sin against the Holy Ghost is to deal with people as though they were things." In any case it is clear from many of the sonnets that the quality in the young man which most disturbed Shakespeare was the prudence of the closed heart.

What of the persons in the plays who were the lords and owners of their faces? Rosencranz and Guildenstern of course; they were the essence of prudent self-interest. Macbeth tried to be, and failed; he was too full of the milk of human kindness. That he failed was his misfortune on the prudential level; on the tragic level it is his glory. Lear and Gloucester were, at the beginning of the play; but their story is their growth in wisdom and warmth. We will look in vain for the type among the heroes, for they are heroes in proportion to their divergence from the type. What of the villains? Well, Edmund is almost a clear case, but he escapes the category by the pleasure he took in being loved. The only major character is Iago, and he, toward the end of the play, becomes the emblem of evil. The purest instance is Northumberland, Hotspur's father, who is motivated by "advised respects" throughout *Richard II* and remains unchanged throughout the two parts of *Henry IV*. He sends his son to death in a vain attempt to secure his own position and later, when still another rebellion is failing, he writes to his fellow rebels letters of "cold intent" announcing his retirement to Scotland. It is his whole character. As Shakespeare conceived the story of *Richard II*, it required an intermediary, a representative of Bolingbroke on whom the

---

[11] Quoted by Donald Stauffer in *The New York Times Book Review*, December 14, 1947.

onus of usurpation would fall, allowing Bolingbroke a measure of integrity. And for this purpose, the creation of a despicable character, he found that the embodiment of the closed heart was what was needed. Later, when even the lesser characters are not so single, the villains are less purely villainous than Northumberland; but to the end a large measure of his soul is the hallmark of their villainy. Shakespeare had feared from the beginning of the sonnets that the young man was cold and self-contained, but it was not until the story was well advanced that the characteristic was clearly recognized, named, and condemned.

All this is far from a simple matter. It involves elements to which few readers will assign precisely the same values. It is further complicated by the young man's being something of a patron of literature in an age of fulsome deference to patrons. Doubtless this contributed to the poet's attitude, but criticism has already made too much of that. A mercenary motive will always be understood, and criticism may seize upon it without the appearance of naïveté. Though this is of great use in simplifying the critic's task, the critic who finds that the author of *King Lear* was primarily an opportunist will also find that his criticism discloses little but himself.

The finest poetry in the sonnets has for its subject the complicated friendship for the young man. It seems to me that this friendship had historical reality, and also that the historicity is not a primary matter. Whether it derives from real or imagined events, the poet's subject matter is his thoughts, emotions, and convictions; and they find expression in poetry through the poet's use of his tradition. Among the relevant aspects of the poet's personality at work here is Shakespeare's gregariousness. It seems that it was with him as with Socrates, who remarked in *Lysis* that while there were many things for which he had no violent desire, he had a passion for friends. This attitude is explicit in the sonnets and implicit in all of Shakespeare's works, as it is in Montaigne's. It would seem to have been in Shakespeare before he read Montaigne, but the priority doesn't matter. A poet adopts an idea because it awakens something in him, because he finds it true, or serviceably so in a germinal way.

Are there not times when even the mature poet is looking for his own thoughts and feelings in those of his fellow writers? And since the thoughts and feelings of an important writer are normally in a state of becoming—sometimes through conscious seeking, sometimes through assimilation, as a seed absorbs its nurture from the earth—we cannot often know what is his and what belongs to his tradition, or that, indeed, they are not the same thing. Granville-Barker has remarked that Shakespeare's writing doubtless taught him as much about people as living among them; that is, his writing required a doubling back on his own experience in order to understand it more fully. As a consequence the literary recreation of an experience may endow the poem with faculties which obscure the germinal experience even to the writer's fellow participants in it.

Like the other ideas common to the sonnets, Shakespeare's ideas of friendship recur throughout his works with a persistence which, for some, will indicate his belief and sketch an aspect of his character. Such readers will say, "Here Shakespeare speaks for himself." And even though they are right, they cannot always hope to convince others of a different persuasion of a matter so individually perceived. They would do better to observe that in by far the greatest number of recurrences the dramatist is setting forth an idea intended, as the dramatic context discloses, to arouse the admiration and sympathy of the audience, and that when the same idea is stated for the same purpose in varying contexts, it becomes apparent that the dramatist holds the idea to be one to which normal humanity will respond with warmth. The sensible man will conclude that it is only a small step from this to the belief that the dramatist responded to the idea in the same way, and that, in fact, he discloses his sympathies in the notions he takes for granted. But we shall do well to remember that the disclosure of such sympathies and thoughts sketches the dramatist's and poet's spiritual biography, or if we prefer a lesser phrase, his poetic personality. The reader cannot proceed from this to the facts of the poet's daily life; not, that is, without some external documentation. Yet what we can learn of Shakespeare from his works, stripped of particulars as it is, is not altogether a dusty answer. Of our friends and neighbors we want to know the facts, for association on the practical level of daily living requires judgments which had better have a factual basis. But of an acquaintance of long ago it is better to know that he had a capacity for loyalty and devotion, and a passion strong enough at times to deny the loyalty, than to know where and when he first encountered his mistress or what her name was. We may know Shakespeare essentially without a bill of particulars, and we may be excused for supposing that, granted the necessity of partial knowledge, we have the best.

It may be that the idea of friendship in the sonnets is an idealization, a purified recreation of the poet's experience, and that it has only a partial or intermittent coincidence with his daily life. Or it may be that Shakespeare came at last to find the idea embodied in a living presence, as Hamlet, knowing an ideal of friendship, found it embodied in Horatio, and henceforth bore them both in his heart's core. We cannot know. We know only that in the sonnets we have a sketch of a troubled friendship in which the poet believes at times that the friend conforms to the ideal, wants at other times to believe it, and fears sometimes that belief is vain.

The Natural Fool of Fortune

To THE Middle Ages, Fortune was the malign goddess who determined the fates of men by spinning her wheel when she would and only because it pleased her to do so. Although this conception of Fortune flourished in Shakespeare's lifetime, it began to lose currency shortly afterwards, in proportion, one supposes, to the spread of education in the modern world. Our own age has transformed her into a prettified version of what she was, Lady Luck, a figure now well on the way to depersonalization. For most modern men her chief reality is one of statistical probability. With Shakespeare it was more accurate to imagine her a person, for so spiteful were the manifestations of chance that they could best be accounted for by assuming the reality of a disposition dominated by conscious and amused malice. It is now common to think of the Elizabethan acceptance of Fortune as appropriate to the more primitive life of that era, as though we were now well on the way to getting things in hand. Shakespeare knew better. His works do not suggest that he was a determinist; one need not be a determinist in order to know the foolishness of a self-centered optimism. In his tragedies it is the villains who assume an unlimited freedom of the will; it is the heroes who come to know better. This is of course a matter of degree. The orthodox view of free will did not suppose that man's powers are uncircumscribed, nor did the fate which Hamlet and Othello came to accept deny all choice. There is rather a conviction of a partial fate, and it is allied to Shakespeare's detestation of the cool prudence discussed in the last chapter. The self-contained man is doubly wrong: he denies his function, and in assuming his power to control, he denies his fate. If one is to live wisely on even a humble level, there must be some recognition of the operation of the

unknowable: "Since why to love I can allege no cause."[1]
In Shakespeare's stories the recognition of the unknowable
is often the beginning of wisdom. We may imagine that
with him this attitude was a generalization from experience,
though we can see its kinship to an older assumption which
placed the beginning of wisdom in "the fear of the Lord."

His attitude toward Fortune is, then, the general attitude
of the perceptive man. For the expression of this attitude
the old concept would, most of the time, do well enough,
although like everything else he took from his tradition it
became in time his own, its coloring and depth of meaning
varying with the context. His use of it in the poems marks
the early stages of his assimilation of it. In *Venus and Adonis*
the only use of "fortune"[2] does not refer to the goddess and
is noteworthy only because it represents the general usage
of the early works. The word is employed in the sense of
"what the future holds in store." It is a common usage, no
more significant than that of the child's story which tells
of a young man who went out into the world to seek his
fortune. The usage, of course, continues, as it does in modern
speech; but a year later in *The Rape of Lucrece* there is also,
for perhaps[3] the first time in Shakespeare, the use of Fortune's wheel. It is found in Lucrece's long reflection[4] on the
existence of evil. It begins,

> Why should the worm intrude the maiden bud?
> Or hateful cuckoos hatch in sparrows' nests?
> Or toads infect fair founts with venom mud?
> Or tyrant folly lurk in gentle breasts?

[1] Sonnet 49.
[2] l. 642.
[3] The precise sequence of Shakespeare's plays is not always to be
determined. The point is that there is no considerable use of the concept of Fortune in *The Comedy of Errors, Two Gentlemen of Verona,
Titus Andronicus*, and *1, 2 Henry VI*.
[4] *The Rape of Lucrece*, 848-973.

The reflection is early in both style and thought. In it Fortune's malice is allied to the depredations of Time, that "ceaseless lackey to eternity," and Time's servant, Opportunity:

> We have no good that we can say is ours,
> But ill-annexed opportunity
> Or kills his life or else his quality.
>
> O opportunity thy guilt is great,
> 'Tis thou that execut'st the traitor's treason. . . .

And so on. There is some justification in these lines for the widely held view, referred to earlier, that Shakespeare tends to consider evil apart from the evildoer. In *Lucrece*, Time, Opportunity, and Fortune are personified abstractions operating on individuals from without. But this is Shakespeare's early view! The passage is, in fact, his first long reflection on evil. There had been the conviction of evil from the beginning, and although in *Lucrece* the awareness of it is more acute, it still has only a tenuous relation to human nature. This is not the mature Shakespeare; it is simply a step on the way to maturity. Later, even as the awareness of extra-human evil deepened, evil is also seen as rooted in man himself:

> Our natures do pursue,
> Like rats that ravin down their proper bane,
> A thirsty evil, and when we drink we die.[5]

However, as he approached thirty there was still a dominant element of impersonality in his thinking about evil. The villains are Time, Opportunity, and Fortune. Time's function is

> To fill with worm-holes stately monuments,
> To feed oblivion with decay of things,
> To blot old books, and alter their contents,
> To pluck the quills from ancient ravens' wings,
> To dry the old oak's sap, and cherish springs;

[5] *Measure for Measure*, 1.2.132-134.

To spoil antiquities of hammer'd steel,
And turn the giddy round of Fortune's wheel.[6]

There is something of this same abstraction in *Romeo and Juliet*, where Romeo, finding the result of his actions to be the opposite of his intention, calls out, "O, I am Fortune's fool!" There is no indication of his personal responsibility in this situation, because, quite simply, he is not viewed as responsible. Nor is there any suggestion of justice; the lovers are "star-crossed" and the reversal of Romeo's fate is an act of Fortune. In a later play Lear too cries out, "I am even the natural fool of Fortune," but in this context the phrase bears a different weight. Here Fortune's malice has a rough relation to the working out of a moral judgment. In short, it is no longer pure malice. In the sonnets the concept of Fortune is more advanced than in *Lucrece*. In Shakespeare's references to the operation of Fortune on him she is thought of as working circumstantially—through his passion for his work and through a social situation. If ever a man had a natural bent for a writer's career, it was Shakespeare; and yet he disliked certain aspects of the writing profession. He was stage-struck, and he could not always be proud of the stage. It is in connection with these matters that he speaks of Fortune in the sonnets. It is also in connection with one aspect or another of his professional life that his references to "slander," "scandal," and "disgrace" are most often allied. Although some of these references are not to our purpose, we shall consider all of them, for so much has been made of them by certain commentators that even a person of small reading about Shakespeare might have gathered that the references suggest something lurid. To ignore some of the references would suggest to some that certain matters were being glossed over in the interest of Shakespeare's good name. It is easy to make too much of these references. One of them

[6] *The Rape of Lucrece*, 946-952.

was the point of departure for Samuel Butler's fantasy in conjectural biography.[7]

There has also been a tendency to overstate their importance to the sonnets themselves. The overstatement arises from the failure to notice that as Shakespeare uses the words they often have a lesser degree of derogation than in modern usage. "Disgraced" in the sonnets means lowered in estimation: "right perfection wrongfully disgrac'd;"[8] and "disgrace" may mean no more than "disfigure" or "obscure," as when the clouds "disgrace" the sun.[9] Or it may mean "discredit"; the poet's lines do him "disgrace" by inadequately expressing his matter.[10] Or the word is used impersonally in connection with beauty[11] or time.[12] On another occasion the poet is "in disgrace with Fortune and men's eyes," which is to say that his social and professional position is far from auspicious. The double use of the word in the eighty-ninth sonnet can best be paraphrased, "You cannot discredit me half as much as I shall discredit myself." The only other occurrence of the word is in the thirty-fourth sonnet, where it indicates the effect of something the young friend had done. The event referred to is unknown, and if it were known, it would contribute chiefly to our knowledge of the youth, for the act was his. As matters stand, the passage tells us something of Shakespeare. It tells us that he regrets a humiliation which continues after the act which caused it has been repented, and that he disapproves of the young man's light assumption that repentance can undo a wrong or its consequences.

The first two uses of "slander" occur in a poem urging that slander does not necessarily indicate a defect in the person slandered, "for slander's mark was ever yet the fair."[13] It is suggested that the slander is an indication of the friend's

[7] *Shakespeare's Sonnets Reconsidered*, first published 1899; present publisher, Jonathan Cape, Thirty Bedford Square, London.
[8] Sonnet 66.   [9] Sonnet 33.   [10] Sonnet 103.
[11] Sonnet 127.   [12] Sonnet 126.   [13] Sonnet 70.

high worth, for in a calumniating world no person of his qualities could escape it. It is a good Shakespearean notion that "virtue itself 'scapes not calumnious strokes,"[14] and that "rumour is a pipe blown by surmises, jealousies, conjectures. . . ."[15] But Shakespeare knew with the rest of mankind that slander can also be provoked, and in the one hundred and thirty-first sonnet it is suggested that the uncomfortable triangular affair had caused some gossip. This is not surprising; an affair such as that depicted by Shakespeare could hardly have failed to cause comment, and the comment is quite explicitly indicated in the sonnets. Shakespeare asks[16] why his "frailties" should be spied on, why the "false adulterate eyes" of others should give "salutation to my sportive blood." He says that in recounting his "abuses" they but "reckon up their own." It is a kind of defense, although the sportive blood is admitted. No doubt such gossip at its height is painful, but one supposes that it was, as in all good societies, a thing which time would cure. The sonnets do not allow us to make the same supposition about the "impression" which "vulgar scandal stamp'd upon my brow."

Of the three words—scandal, slander, and disgrace—"scandal" is by far the strongest in Shakespeare's usage, and his use of it in connection with the theatre is in precise conformity to an old tradition. Opposition to the theatre has an ancient history, and in the first centuries of the Christian era was not unjustified. Until the sixth century actors were pagans and the stage was dedicated to idolatry. There were soon changes, but the attitude toward the theatre changed less than the theatre itself. It had been held by St. John Chrysostom (fourth century) that the spectators shared with the actors in the iniquity of the theatre,[17] for if there were

---

[14] *Hamlet*, 1.3.38.
[15] *King Henry the Fourth*, part two, Induction.　　[16] Sonnet 121.
[17] See *The Stage Controversy in France from Corneille to Rousseau*. M. Barras, Publications of the Institute of French Studies, Inc., New York, 1933.

devoted to the ill-repute his theatrical career brought him.
They begin,

> Alas! 'tis true I have gone here and there,
> And made myself a motley to the view,
> Gor'd mine own thoughts, sold cheap what is most dear....

He seems to say, "I have not only acted in plays, I have
written them, exposing to public view my most private
thoughts, selling for money what is beyond price." It is sometimes held that "motley" does not necessarily refer to the
theatre, but the next sonnet puts the matter beyond doubt:

> O, for my sake do you with Fortune chide,
> The guilty goddess of my harmful deeds,
> That did not better for my life provide
> Than public means which public manners breeds.
> Thence comes it that my name receives a brand,
> And almost thence my nature is subdu'd
> To what it works in, like the dyer's hand:
> Pity me then, and wish I were renew'd....

The attitude here expressed is often distasteful to those
who love the theatre, and welcome to those who do
not; but it need not trouble the first, and it should not
give pleasure to the others, for it does not express Shakespeare's total attitude toward his craft. It could only be total
—as it often is!—for the hack writer, the man whose relation
to his craft, no matter how habitual, is promiscuous. Such a
person is likely to feel that he is engaging in something
unworthy of him, a feeling which may or may not be justified. It may be that the advertising firm for which he works,
or his studio, or the editor who buys his stuff, honors him
in accepting what he produces. Still, if he has other ambi-
tions, or if the milieu in which he lives is not *en rapport*
with his market, he will feel that his better nature is betrayed. The sense of writing in an unworthy cause is a common one. Many a dramatist working in Hollywood feels

as Shakespeare felt during his early days in London. At that time the Elizabethan theatre was a growing institution of tremendous potentialities, but though, like the early movies, it was popular, it was not accepted, and a career in it was not a matter for pride.

Given a profession of ill-repute, the sense of self-betrayal in it is all the more likely in a man whose relation to his craft is not wholly commercial. But with him the feeling is not total. To him his craft is also his means of saying what he must say. This he regards as worthy, and his response to his profession is complicated by it. With him the common condition is one of mingled devotion and distaste—and it is never more common than with those who write for the theatre. Dramatists like actors and singers are forever retiring; they escape, and they return. Shakespeare himself retired at about forty-five, but he went back from time to time.

In moving from Stratford to London the young Shakespeare had changed worlds and, more important, social levels. In the more homogeneous life of Stratford his family had had a reputable position. To be sure it had fallen into poor circumstances by the time of his adolescence, but that is the sort of change which does little to alter a family's self-view. Quite the contrary! In any case he had moved from one milieu into another in which he was not at ease in his struggle for acceptance. In 1592 Robert Greene, a fellow dramatist, thought of him as an unproved interloper. His phrase for Shakespeare was "an upstart crow beautified with our feathers." Situations such as that in which Shakespeare found himself are common enough in literary history, and for the young writer of stature and integrity the situation need not be all loss. It is doubtful if the world's important work is ever done by those who are perfectly adjusted to their environment and are at peace with themselves. Although the artist's sense of difference from the social norm may be responsible for much that is neurotic in modern art, it is probable that without some measure of difference there would be no art at all—at least no art of importance. Gide's self-preoccupation has led to much that is revealing, not only of himself but of mankind. On 7 January 1924 he recorded the following sentences in his journal: "The desire to depict from nature the people one has met . . . turns to account a certain gift of the eye and of the pen. But the creation of new people becomes a natural need only in those who are tormented by imperious inner complexity and are not satisfied with their own deeds." This states briefly much that psychology has to say on the matter, and it is germane to what Shakespeare says in the sonnets: there is his depiction of his discontent in his love for the dark lady; his complex view of his friendship with the young man, a rewarding relationship seldom free from distrust; his references to events which cause him embarrassment; his dislike of certain aspects of his profession and his recurrent dissatisfaction with his writings. If his failure to be satisfied with his writings were not explicit in the sonnets, it could be inferred from his refusal throughout his life to repeat his successes. If the sonnets to the young man were not a revelation of the poet's inner complexity, we would know it from the plays, where the revelation is found to be in rough proportion to the greatness of the work.

Apart from all this, Shakespeare was aware of an indecency inherent in the practice of literature. He felt that it involved a certain violation of privacy. Though the feeling is not common to all writers, it is far from rare, and with those who share the feeling, it exists, one supposes, in proportion to their sensibility. The writer may harden himself to it, coming in time to believe, like Mrs. Trollope, that if his use of his friends is skillful enough, no one will recognize the pigs in the sausage. The evidence other writers have left us on this matter indicates that self-exposure cannot always be circumvented or rationalized with like ease. Browning's statement that if Shakespeare had unlocked his heart in the

sonnets, he was less Shakespearean than he should have been
—"the less Shakespeare he"—means among other things that
Browning could not bear to be a writer without a mask, and
that he attributed a degree of the same sensitivity to Shakespeare. One may find exaggeration without denying the re-
siduum of truth in Shakespeare's repeated statements that
the self-revelation of his poems was embarrassing. Here and
there his plays disclose his reflections on the subject. When
Touchstone instructs Audrey on literature, she says, "I do not
know what 'poetical' is. Is it honest in deed and word?"[20]
Of his own writings he says, "I am sham'd by that which
I bring forth. . . ."[21] It is only a partial view, but it is surely
a genuine revelation of his attitude toward his work. With
Shakespeare it arises from the consciousness of his theatre
and his place in it, from the embarrassment of self-revelation,
and from the discrepancy between his early conceptions and
his realization of them. This is of course only an aspect of
Shakespeare's self-view, but it is one to which he testifies,
and one which on a priori grounds is probable enough. It
is a matter of long record that depression can be a prime
subject for and spur to poetical composition, and those of us
who are not poets can only suppose that the melancholy,
sometimes intensified for purposes of composition, is released,
at least in part, by the act of creation. A man of normal self-
awareness cannot be altogether miserable while writing well.
Arnold must have known an excellence other than love while
writing *Dover Beach*, and Shakespeare's lines expressing
devotion and embarrassment do not express his whole view
of the situation.

The sonnets certify that he was not always discouraged
and that the intensity of the discouragement, when it existed,
was not constant. Usually the friendship is regarded as a
compensation for the ills the poet endured. The best expression of the compensatory aspect of the friendship is the

[20] *As You Like It*, 3.3.18.   [21] Sonnet 72.

twenty-ninth sonnet. In it the unestablished writer, finding himself unfavored of Fortune and without the hoped-for approval of his fellow men, wishes he were more like the friend—that he had more cause for hope, were more handsome, had more friends, and that he had this man's craftsmanship and that man's range. But when he is least contented by what he most enjoys (that is, his work), the recollection of the friend takes him out of himself, and he is at ease:

> When in disgrace with Fortune and men's eyes,
> I all alone beweep my outcast state,
> And trouble deaf heaven with my bootless cries,
> And look upon myself and curse my fate,
> Wishing me like to one more rich in hope,
> Featur'd like him, like him with friends possess'd,
> Desiring this man's art and that man's scope,
> With what I most enjoy contented least;
> Yet in these thoughts myself almost despising,
> Haply I think on thee,—and then my state,
> Like to the lark at break of day arising
> From sullen earth sings hymns at heaven's gate;
>> For thy sweet love remember'd such wealth brings
>> That then I scorn to change my state with kings.

Perhaps it is worth observing that the release from depression is expressed through the image of the lark, a remembrance of earlier days when the cares of his London career were unknown; and it is called into being by the recollection of a friendship in contrast to the insecurity of his existence, his awareness of his unrealized powers, and all those aspects of his life to which "slander," "disgrace," and "scandal" refer. There is for the moment one person with whom his good name is secure—as secure, that is, as it may be in a world clouded with mutability. But his views on "good name" will be the subject of the next chapter.

Reputation and the Knowledge of Good

L IKE the other convictions basic to Shakespeare's writings, the view of reputation seems to have been present from the beginning and to have taken on new associations as he matured, so that in the later works it does not stand alone and cannot be estimated in isolation from correlative thoughts and attitudes. Perhaps the most striking quality of his mature art is its simultaneousness. Other poet-dramatists, at least for the purposes of a given work, are content to view life from a vantage point. Shakespeare always wants to see it whole—therefore the juxtapositions and complexities which so disturb readers of a neo-classical turn of mind, who, in our day, assume as dogma the canons which have no authority beyond personal preference. For the past three decades we have been told that *Hamlet* is a failure, and when pressed for reasons the advocates of this notion reply that it is the function of art to clarify life, and that *Hamlet* fails because it is not sufficiently clear. To this it is possible to reply, "But what if Shakespeare's version of the Hamlet story could not have been made as clear as you want it without falsifying the view of life which it embodies?" Or one is told that the characterization of Cleopatra is too varied, too complex. Is there then some recognized limit to the knowledge of humanity that a tragedy may disclose? The primary difference between such criticism and the criticism of Thomas Rymer is Rymer's greater self-knowledge and the then acknowledged tradition in which he wrote.

Shakespeare's mature work is multi-faceted, and this, surely, is its hallmark. Is it not the inexhaustibility of Hamlet and Cleopatra which does most to mark them off from the characterizations of other writers at their best? Everybody knows them, millions know them well, but no sensible person supposes that he knows all there is to know about them. Is it not the simultaneousness of *King Lear* which, as much as anything else, keeps it fresh? It is possible to be tired of *King Lear* after editing or acting it, but it is not possible to be tired of *King Lear* for long. Its complexities and rich juxtapositions are always capable of new meanings and new insights.

Although creation of this sort is a power which came slowly to Shakespeare, it is not reserved for his greatest works. On a smaller scale it began to emerge as the hallmark of his work as soon as he had mastered the means of revealing it. It is manifest in scenes which, curiously enough, have been most often praised for their simplicity. Let us turn to a scene written just after he had passed his apprentice period. The opening scene of the final act of *The Merchant of Venice* serves chiefly to return the play to the romance with which it began. In it two pairs of newly-married lovers are reunited *away from* the scene of Shylock's villainy. We are at Belmont again, and the scene opens with the moonlit dialogue of Lorenzo and Jessica, which is interrupted first by the messenger and then by the clown, and when the lovers are alone again we hear these words:

> How sweet the moonlight sleeps upon this bank!
> Here will we sit and let the sound of music
> Creep into our ears: soft stillness and the night
> Become the touches of sweet harmony.
> Sit, Jessica. Look how the floor of heaven
> Is thick inlaid with patens of bright gold.
> There's not the smallest orb which thou behold'st
> But in his motion like an angel sings,
> Still quiring to the young-eyed cherubins;
> Such harmony is in immortal souls;
> But whilst this muddy vesture of decay
> Doth grossly close it in, we cannot hear it.

There follows the well-known passage on music. Then Portia arrives, remarking to Nerissa as she enters,

> That light we see is burning in my hall.
> How far that little candle throws his beams,[1]
> So shines a good deed in a naughty world.

It is all wonderful and quite gratuitous. With a lesser dramatist, with, say, a master of the well-made play, it would have been quite impossible, perhaps even unimaginable; for what storyteller of any singleness of purpose would have complicated the romance of young love with a reference to the body as "this muddy vesture of decay"? And without Shakespeare's mastery of his poetic medium, how could the lines be spoken, as they clearly are, without the slightest diminution of the romance? It was possible only because Shakespeare was then entering his artistic maturity and had come by the technique by which the associations natural to him could be stated. Beauty, love, mutability, and the truth that lies beyond the flesh are all thought of together, and followed by Portia's remark on the circumscribed effectiveness of moral good. What is peculiarly Shakespearean about these lines is that no one of the ideas glanced at decreases the others. Quite the contrary! With Shakespeare the awareness of the transience of things urges deeper appreciation, and the knowledge of the constricting limitations of the body reinforces the awareness of its good. There is nothing in Shakespeare's plays at all like the close of Chaucer's *Troilus and Criseyde,* where Troilus, having mounted to the eighth sphere, looks down on "this litel spot of erthe" and laughs

---

[1] The two quartos and the folio each place a comma after "beams." The exclamation point of all modern texts is thus without authority and represents nothing but an intrusion of the editors' greater cheerfulness. The text clearly means a good deed in a bad world shines no more brightly than a little candle. This is made doubly apparent by the speech which follows: "When the moon shone we did not see the candle."

inwardly at the grief of those who mourn his death, know-ing at last that in respect to eternal felicity all earthly things are vain.

The end of Chaucer's poem is a magnificent conclusion to what I take to be the best narrative poem in the language, and it represents one of the ways in which grandeur may be achieved. The point here is that it was not Shakespeare's way. Even when he is most aware of evil, the world still has its good. With him, too, "the glory of the celestial is one, and the glory of the terrestrial is another." And they are coexist-ent. The horror of mutability, the love of earth, the regard for the good opinion of his peers—these stand together and support each other. His tragedies, though Christian in point of view, have a secular frame of reference. They find their good in the world, as the regard of Hamlet and Othello for their good name among men testifies. It is sometimes said that in the "Come let's away to prison" speech Lear re-nounces the world, but the notion is only partly true. Lear is renouncing the world as he has known it in order to find, as he thinks, contentment in the love of Cordelia. And that is Christian too. It does not exhaust Christianity, but it is Christian, and it is compatible with those aspects of Christi-anity which normally lie beyond Shakespeare's range. I think a recognition of this is important.

I do not know why obvious things should be so little recognized or so easily forgotten. Perhaps after we have worn our sophistication and our philosophy a little longer we shall one day come to terms with them. On that day we shall be both less sophisticated and wiser, and we shall be nearer Shakespeare, for he is not afraid to accept without con-descension what everyone knows. Beauty is good, and so is poetry, and love, and children, and friendship, and the good opinion of one's friends. And they are associated goods. I imagine that something quite like his view of reputation is one of the motives animating even the critics who deprecate his view of it. Instances of this deprecation are multitudinous. We shall consider only one, a criticism of *Othello* written from a point of view which finds itself esthetically, religiously (and I think unnecessarily) incompatible with the play. But let us first recall the lines criticized:

> Soft you, a word or two before you go.
> I have done the state some service, and they know't.
> No more of that. I pray you, in your letters,
> When you shall these unlucky deeds relate,
> Speak of me as I am; nothing extenuate,
> Nor set down aught in malice. Then must you speak
> Of one that lov'd not wisely but too well;
> Of one not easily jealous, but being wrought
> Perplex'd in the extreme; of one whose hand,
> Like the base Indian, threw a pearl away
> Richer than all his tribe; of one whose subdu'd eyes,
> Albeit unus'd to the melting mood,
> Drop tears as fast as the Arabian trees
> Their medicinal gum. Set you down this;
> And say besides, that in Aleppo once,
> Where a malignant and a turban'd Turk
> Beat a Venetian and traduc'd the state,
> I took by the throat the circumcised dog,
> And smote him, thus. [*Stabs himself.*]

Our most distinguished living critic and poet is able to say of these lines: "What Othello seems to me to be doing in making this speech is *cheering himself up*. He is endeavouring to escape reality, he has ceased to think about Desdemona, and is thinking about himself. Humility is the most difficult of all virtues to achieve; nothing dies harder than the desire to think well of oneself. Othello succeeds in turning himself into a pathetic figure, by adopting an *aesthetic* rather than a moral attitude, dramatizing himself against his environment. He takes in the spectator, but the human motive is primarily to take in himself."[2] Surely not everyone is obliged to concur in this view of the scene. Mr. Eliot's view proceeds from a belief which is both implicit and explicit in his works, that we like others to think well of us because we want to think well of ourselves; and it is taken that, human nature being what it is, any favorable view of it is a rationalization. I do not suppose that the view of human depravity disclosed by Eliot's works is stronger than that disclosed by Shakespeare's. The difference is that Eliot's view seems to comprehend all of life, and Shakespeare's manifestly does not. With Shakespeare's characters there is always the possibility of doing good, and of knowing what they do. Surely humility does not require that our minds be cabbages and that we do good only without knowing it. If it is a sin to know what we do, I trust that we may be forgiven for hoping that the sin is not mortal. Of course we must recognize the humility of the saint, who rejects his fame for himself while knowing that it redounds to the glory of God, but there is no need to consider Othello on that level. Indeed, any such consideration of him violates the whole context of the play. Viewing the play on a sub-saintly level, one might validly object to Othello's suicide on grounds both Christian and pagan, but that is not Mr. Eliot's point. Apparently he would prefer to have Othello kill himself while thinking of Desdemona in an agony of self-reproach, but that would be too simple psychologically for Shakespeare's purpose, and much too romantic. In any case Mr. Eliot's remarks are not relevant to the work of a writer who believes in his heart that there is a terrestrial glory. To the man who loves the work of such a writer, *Hamlet* appears to be the most successful play in the history of western civilization. Now in the fourth century of its existence, it is more widely read, more often acted, more often translated, than

[2] T. S. Eliot, *Shakespeare and the Stoicism of Seneca*, Oxford University Press, London, 1927.

any other play in English or any other language. To Mr. Eliot it is a failure. To the point of view which considers *Hamlet* a failure, the fame of the play obviously cannot indicate either its success or its worth, but for the sublunary reader it will serve. Shakespeare never forsook his faith in the good opinion of man.

It should be remembered that with Shakespeare reputation is not impersonal. It is at times identified with honor and is most often used to indicate a status with a limited group of men, or with men of a given level. Sometimes it is even used to indicate status with an individual. Cassio's misdemeanor costs him his lieutenancy, but when he grieves for his lost reputation—"I have lost the immortal part of myself, and what remains is bestial"—he is thinking, among other things, of Othello's estimate of him which reflects his integrity as a man. Although what Shakespeare has to say about reputation is clear enough, we sometimes misunderstand his statements because we are not willing to see the assumptions behind them. Today the word "character" is used to indicate what a man is, "reputation" to indicate what others take him to be; and thus a concern with reputation has come to suggest a specious preoccupation with appearances. With Shakespeare the connotations were in general reversed. "Character" with him means either letters and figures or an outward sign of an inner reality, but not, as with us, the reality itself. With him, as with us, a man's reputation may be good or bad, and it goes without saying that reputation is not always justly bestowed; but he also uses "reputation" to mean credit and honor, much as seventeenth-century France used the word "gloire," much, indeed, as the translators of St. Augustine use the word "glory" in *The City of God*. The devil is citing scripture for his own purposes when Iago makes the speech on good name. With Shakespeare the opinions a man's peers hold of him are taken to be an index of his worth and the primary reward of his most serious strivings. Conversely, he associates the absence of such opinions with despair. Macbeth in his desolation knew that he "must not look to have" "honour, love, obedience, troops of friends"; and with that realization there came another: "I have liv'd long enough." One of the arguments used by Ulysses in urging Achilles to action was that

> . . . no man is lord of anything,
> Though in and of him there be much consisting,
> Till he communicate his parts to others:
> Nor doth he of himself know them for aught
> Till he behold them formed in the applause
> Where they're extended. . . .[3]

It is a familiar concept in Shakespeare, and an awareness of it is basic to an understanding of him. In the plays of the tragic period it is more richly full than in the sonnets, but even there it was fully formed. When the poet says that he must strive to know his "shames and praises" from the lips of his friend,[4] he intends it quite literally. For him the friend's opinion is the external assurance of the reality of a personal faith.

There is even one occasion in the sonnets when an evil reputation unjustly bestowed is said to be worse than the evil itself, since the accused person pays the price of evil without even the fleeting reward of the wrongdoer's illicit pleasure:

> 'Tis better to be vile than vile esteem'd,
> When not to be receives reproach of being;
> And the just pleasure lost, which is so deem'd
> Not by our feeling, but by others' seeing. . . .[5]

Perhaps Shakespeare would not have written these lines during the tragic period, for in the work of that time the overwhelming emphasis is on the reality of good and evil

---

[3] *Troilus and Cressida*, 3.3.115-120.
[4] Sonnet 112.   [5] Sonnet 121.

as distinct from the appearance of them. But speculation on what he could or would have written is not of much use. He is a poet and playwright, not a philosopher or a theologian, and he cannot be held to systems of thought. One must recognize—and not be surprised at the recognition—that the sonnet under discussion is, for want of a better word, quite pagan. And we should notice that although it is Shakespeare's only commitment to a pragmatic ethics, it follows from his conviction of the value of reputation and is at the very least not alien to an aspect of his view of evil to which we shall shortly turn. We must, too, avoid even appearing to apologize for the doctrine of a poem, or altering it in any way. We may take it that it expresses what for the moment he felt to be true. The honest critic, like the good poet who aims at a comprehensive depiction of mankind, must have a certain affinity for chaos: he must stand by his perceptions; he must not deny them in favor of what he feels he ought to see, or what he thinks the author ought to have written.

The theme of the sonnet is related to another aspect of Shakespeare's view of life which we have had occasion to mention before. It is the knowledge that nothing, not even evil, is of necessity completely evil, for some good may come of it. Since a cloistered virtue is never complete, and since mankind is famously susceptible to evil, the Shakespearean man is confronted with a perpetual dilemma—he can achieve maturity of spirit only at the risk of infection. Yet the infection need not be fatal. The sinner may follow Hamlet's advice:

> confess yourself to heaven,
> Repent what's past, avoid what is to come. . . .[6]

Or, learning through experience, he may grow in stature, becoming stronger in virtue and wisdom through the knowledge of evil.

---

[6] *Hamlet*, 3.4.149.

With Shakespeare's greatest works, as with the Dostoevsky of *Crime and Punishment*, the knowledge of good is won through suffering and sin. One thinks of Shaw's English chaplain, who had no real knowledge of evil until he had shared in it by assisting at the burning of Joan of Arc: "I had not seen it, you know. That is the great thing: you must see it. And then you are redeemed and saved." And when he was asked if the sufferings of Our Lord had not been enough for him, he replied, "No. Oh no; not at all. I had seen them in pictures, and read of them in books, and been greatly moved by them, as I thought. But it was no use. . . ." Redemption through a knowledge of evil is at the heart of Shakespeare's deepest revelations of man. He presents it in pagan and Christian contexts. It may lead to repentance and confession, as with Hamlet's mother; or to repentance and prayer, as with Lear, even though Lear's gods are pagan gods; or it may lead a character to esteem honor and justice above salvation, as with Othello; or to a knowledge of evil without repentance, as with Macbeth. But it is the heart of the matter with all of them. In the dark lady sonnets, lust does not reveal its nature until after indulgence, and its slow repletion and recognition are one.

The idea is one of Shakespeare's most pervasive convictions. He relates it not only to moral matters but to those more commonly thought to fall within the realm of manners, and to the indeterminate area between manners and morals:

> O benefit of ill! now I find true
> That better is by evil still made better;
> And ruin'd love when it is built anew,
> Grows fairer than at first, more strong, far greater.[7]

The following sonnet begins with, "That you were once unkind befriends me now," and it concludes with the hope

[7] Sonnet 119.

that each would be ransomed by the trespass of the other. In another sonnet[8] he discovers that "worse essays prov'd thee my best of love." Evil of all degrees may come at last to good. This is not at all the "cheerful faith" of later eras "that all which we behold is full of blessings." It is rather the knowledge that in the face of whatever evil there may be, there is still the universal potential for good. There is the belief in the reality of good and evil, and the knowledge that although the forces of evil are numerous and often dominant, good may assert itself, sometimes even through the agency of evil.

It will be granted that this is not a simple view, but one does not look for simplicity in literature which does not evade profundity or the mystery or paradox to which profundity at times conducts us. On the dramatic level the expression of the view is saved from the danger of chaos by Shakespeare's belief in reputation and his denial of relativism. The denial, always assumed, is explicitly stated in *Troilus and Cressida*, where the Trojans, faced with the ultimatum of the Greeks, are debating their course of action. Troilus supports his position by arguing that everything is relative. "What is aught but as 'tis valued?" is the way he puts it. Hector replies that moral values are absolute:

> . . . value dwells not in particular will;
> It holds his estimate and dignity
> As well wherein 'tis precious of itself
> As in the prizer. . . .
> And the will dotes that is inclinable
> To what infectiously itself affects,
> Without some image of the affected merit.[9]

This is not Shakespeare's most felicitous writing, but a little study will show its meaning to be indisputably clear. Essentially it says that the moral value of an action is inherent in the act, and that it is madness to rationalize individual desire into precept and equate it with value known on other grounds. This, moreover, is the central theme of the play. The point for the moment is that Shakespeare is forever saying that actions have inherent values and that a certain agreement in the recognition of these values is the assurance of their existence. The Christian reader of Shakespeare who has an unshaken faith in revelation will find this assurance unnecessary, but he need not find Shakespeare's use of it inconsistent with the dogma he accepts.

In the same scene, Hector, in defense of his position, appeals to the authority of "these moral laws of nature and of nations." His point of view, which is also Shakespeare's, is precisely parallel to certain aspects of the contemporary concept of law. Divine law was the will of God made manifest by revelation. Natural law was the will of God made manifest in nature. Human law was law as discovered by mankind, and it was agreed that human law was valid in proportion to its approximation of natural law. This concept of law was an inheritance from the Middle Ages, and in England between Shakespeare and the Middle Ages the concept was never forsaken. It was not even denied by the lawyers of Henry VIII in his long struggle with the papacy. We should remember that the men of the Middle Ages never spoke of "making" a law; they always "found" one. It was always *presumed to exist in nature*. Now, apart from divine revelation (and natural law exists apart from revelation by definition), there could be no assurance of the validity of justice beyond the agreement of competent men, whose competence was not determined by popular vote or by their approximation to a majority. It is to this reliance on agreement that Shakespeare's faith in reputation is related.

In our own time and country we say that a man has a "right" to a certain belief or proposed course of action. We do not legally justify the right by religious sanction or say that it exists in nature; we simply take it *as given*—we do not ask by whom or by what. For instance, we take it as self-evident that men "are and ought to be free," and we proceed to formulate laws guaranteeing that freedom. These laws can exist only as long as we are agreed on the truth of what is *taken as given*. It is obvious that the agreement is not necessarily unanimous. It appears from this that we are not altogether different from Shakespeare in our dependence upon assumptions, for, apart from divine revelation or our unquestioning acceptance of human authority (which in secular law at our time would lead to a species of dictatorship), the only test of belief other than that of private intuition is the agreement of competent men. We like to think that we are committed to the pragmatic test, that we accept a thing because it works; and with respect to material matters our self-estimate is beyond dispute. But in the realm of moral behavior, which is the realm Shakespeare is concerned with, the pragmatic test could only resort to evidence provided by some degree of agreement, and we should again find ourselves Shakespeare's neighbors.

Appendix

Evidence and Two Shakespearean Fallacies

SINCE this study has rejected the now widely spread notion that Shakespeare's sonnets to the young man reflect a homosexual relationship with him, it might be well to state in an appendix the reasons for the rejection, lest the reader suppose that the question has not been faced. Unfortunately the matter cannot be discussed briefly. The question is basically one of the value of evidence, and the evidence offered by the sonnets is of a kind which cannot be described without reference to other categories of evidence. Since I should like to suggest to the general reader a reasonable procedure which he might follow in thinking about this and kindred matters, I begin this essay with another Shakespearean misconception. This will allow me to establish the bases of the procedure, and it will, I hope, allow the reader to get both misconceptions "out of the way at one time and be no more plagued and pestered with them. . . ."

We all tend to find in a writer what we know to be there; and since a certain knowledge of Shakespeare is a part of the heritage of all English-speaking people, the reader is likely to approach Shakespeare with certain predispositions which he finds it pleasant to justify. What the reader knows about his author may or may not be true; but true or false his reading will be influenced by what he knows. If he has been told that the sonnets to the young man celebrate a homosexual episode in Shakespeare's life, he will, if he has not rejected the notion, respond to the poems in a manner very different from that of the man to whom the idea has not occurred. Perhaps it is not too much to say that in our time the moderately well-read reader cannot understand the sonnets until he has come to grips with the problem of their alleged homosexuality.

Misconception grows because various bits of evidence, or what looks like evidence, are given more than their proper weight. The error to which mankind is most prone is to ignore a fact in favor of an hypothesis. "It is the nature of an hypothesis," wrote Tristram Shandy in an attempt to explain how his father came by some of his more preposterous ideas, "when once a man has conceived it, that it assimilates everything to it as proper nourishment, and, from the moment of your begetting it, it generally grows bigger by everything you see, hear, read, or understand."[1] There could be no better description of the way in which the most monstrous nonsense about Shakespeare comes into being, and there is no greater nonsense than Baconianism, the cult which supposes that the works of Shakespeare were written by Sir Francis Bacon or some other worthy. It is the most widespread fallacy in the diverse field of Shakespeare studies, and it is, moreover, the archetype of the others. Whether it functions in favor of Bacon, Oxford, Derby, or Dyer, it functions in the same way and on the same assumptions.

Let it be understood that this is not addressed to the confirmed Baconian. He cannot be converted from his ways. If he says a thing three times, it is true. Besides, though he is vulnerable, he is not assailable, for his arguments present nothing to challenge but assertion. He is a zealot whose cult is without dogma, reason, or revelation. There is simply belief, and when pure belief is sincerely held it is idle to question it. It was Mark Twain who once remarked after a performance of *Romeo and Juliet*, "That is about the best play that Lord Bacon ever wrote." He will serve as an example. A former solicitor-general of the United States, James Montgomery Beck[2] tells of a discussion of Baconianism

---

[1] Lawrence Sterne, *Tristram Shandy*, book 2, chapter 19.

[2] James Montgomery Beck, Foreword (xx-xxi) *Links between Shakespeare and the Law*, Sir Dunbar Plunket Barton, Faber and Gwyer, Limited, London, 1928.

he once had with Twain when visiting in his home: "As the discussion proceeded, I naturally suggested some of the many arguments which, if documentary history has any value, support the claims of the Stratford poet. The more I submitted the arguments for his consideration, the more passionate his temper became. At first I regarded this with some amusement, but later with some concern. Finally, when I advanced some argument to which he could not give even a plausible answer, he suddenly burst into a volley of profanity, worthy of his early days on the Mississippi, and cursed and reviled Shakespeare with a coarseness of phrase that would have done justice to Falstaff and his companions. After this explosion, he sullenly went into the billiard-room and commenced to knock the balls idly about, while I went up to my room and considered whether I should pack my valises and make my adieux. We met at dinner, but nothing was said about the disputed question, nor in the few remaining days of my visit. On the following morning we took a long walk over the hills of Connecticut, and no one could have been more delightful than Mark Twain. . . . I gained a clearer idea of his original and, generally, noble mind than I had at any previous time, but neither of us ventured to refer again to the controversial subject."

At first it appears difficult to see why people should be attracted to this belief; but a man must believe something, and a belief in a heterodox doctrine involving no obligations has the double charm of novelty and irresponsibility. When to these is added the comfort of unconscious snobbery, the appeal is apparent. So, at any rate, a long history would indicate, for Shakespeare is not the only author whose works have been attributed without evidence to other men, and the basic arguments for the attributions have been the same for almost two thousand years. Because Terence was thought to have been born a slave, it was supposed by some that he could not have written like a patrician, and his works were from time to time attributed to other men, chiefly to Scipio Africanus. Quintilian[3] remarks on the attribution but does not subscribe to it. By the time of the Renaissance the belief had considerable currency. Both Montaigne[4] and Roger Ascham[5] held it. Ascham could not believe that the eloquence of certain Terentian scenes was the work of one born a "servile stranger." In another connection the same patrician assumption appears in Montaigne, when he says that he would not believe that Caesar had written the works known to be his if there were not also the records of Caesar's deeds. The assumption is clear: it is taken that literary excellence is a function of breeding or social status, or at the least of distinction in some nonliterary field. A general may write well, or a patrician; but not a man of ordinary family or profession—not, for instance, an actor. The attitude toward Terence is precisely parallel to the Baconian's attitude toward Shakespeare.

The first suggestion that Bacon wrote the works of Shakespeare was made by Herbert Lawrence in 1769 in *The Life and Adventures of Common Sense*. Although the suggestion was repeated by J. C. Hart in *The Romance of Yachting* in 1848, it received little attention until a decade later, when W. H. Smith in England·(*Was Bacon the Author of Shakespeare's Plays?* 1856, and *Bacon and Shakespeare*, 1857) and Delia Bacon in America (*The Philosophy of the Plays of Shakespeare Unfolded*, 1857) once more argued the case in

---

[3] Quintilian, *Institutio Oratorio*, 10, 1, 99.

[4] Montaigne, *Essays*, "A Consideration Upon Cicero." "And if perfection of well-speaking might bring any glorie sutable unto a great personage, Scipio and Lelius would never have resigned the honour of their comedies, and the elegancies and smooth-sportfull conceits of the Latine tongue, unto an Affrican servant. . . . I could hardly be removed from this opinion." Florio's translation.

[5] Roger Ascham, *The School Master*, second part, section on *Imitatio*. ". . . it is well known by good record of learning, and that by Cicero's own witness, that some of the comedies bearing Terence's name were written by the worthy Scipio and the wise Laelius. . . ."

favor of Bacon. By that time the temper of the age had changed, and the state of thinking about Shakespeare was such as to make the argument in favor of Bacon plausible to certain people. The acceptance of the belief is, in fact, the outgrowth of Romantic and Victorian attitudes toward Shakespeare. The separation of the writer and his works came about through the magnification of Shakespeare's worth as a writer and the deprecation of his worth as a man, a dichotomy recorded by the foremost writers of the Victorian age. The writers of the Romantic period liked to emphasize Shakespeare's original genius by contrasting his literary achievement with his middle-class circumstances. The Victorians carried the matter further, until the praise of Shakespeare's genius became a magnificat. To Carlyle "Shakespeare and Dante are saints of poetry; really if we think about it, canonized, so that it is impiety to meddle with them. . . . They dwell apart, in a kind of royal solitude; none equal, none second to them."[6] And in one respect Shakespeare is the greater: "He is the greatest of intellects." To Emerson he is "as much out of the category of eminent authors, as he is out of the crowd. He is inconceivably wise; the others, conceivably. A good reader can, in a sort, nestle into Plato's brain, and think from thence; but not into Shakespeare's. . . ."[7] And even Arnold, in his sonnet on Shakespeare, finds him great beyond human comprehension. All this, of course, is admirably motivated. He *is* the greatest of English dramatists and poets, and we owe him our praise; but there is little homage in praising him for what he is not. He is a thinker, but he is not in any considerable sense an original thinker, and the magnitude of his genius is incomprehensible only in the way in which genius of the first order is always staggering.

[6] Thomas Carlyle, *On Heroes and Hero-Worship*, "The Hero as Poet."

[7] Ralph Waldo Emerson, *Representative Men*, "Shakespeare."

The Victorians created for Shakespeare a greatness beyond human achievement and then noticed that their creation was incompatible, not with humanity, but with a man of Shakespeare's background and profession. Emerson could not reconcile Shakespeare's genius as a poet with his having been "a jovial actor and manager." He could not believe that he had used "his genius for the public amusement." There is little in this more harmful than Emerson's priestly solemnity and the condescension to the theatre which flourished in his time, but for the moment let us content ourselves with the discrepancy between what he had made of Shakespeare the poet and what he took Shakespeare the man to be. Other Victorians of less democratic principles shared Emerson's solemnity and distaste for actors, and they reflected further that Shakespeare was of the middle classes and seems to have had no very constant regard for propriety. His marriage, for instance, was not quite regular. In this they were quite right, and quite wrong, of course, in supposing it to have any relevance to his powers as a writer. The simple truth is that in England the peaks of literary greatness have been bourgeois from the beginning. The exceptions are more apparent than actual. Tennyson was a poet before he was Lord Tennyson, and since Byron's title came upon him unexpectedly, there had been little in his early training to prepare him for it. But the peaks of greatness—Chaucer, Spenser, Shakespeare, Milton, and so on down through the years— were all middle class. There is no basis whatever for supposing literary greatness to be incompatible with a man of Shakespeare's station.

As for the vulgarity in Shakespeare's works, respectable people throughout the century had been hoping that he had not written *that*. Coleridge supposed that the remarks of the porter in *Macbeth* on drink and lechery had been inserted into the play. The point of view may be described simply: it was decided that what was objectionable in Shakespeare had been written by somebody else. This left Shakespeare the unsullied poet as divinity, and it soon became apparent that he could not also have been that man from Stratford. Having divided Shakespeare in two, the writer and the man, some of the Victorians were ready to cast about for a more likely candidate to whom the works could be attributed, and they were content to seize upon the proposals put forth in the articles by Miss Bacon and Smith. Bacon was not as honest as the man from Stratford seems to have been, he had written just enough verses to demonstrate that he was not a poet; but he was a distinguished man—Francis Bacon, Baron Verulam and Viscount St. Albans—he had been to the university, he was a man of letters, and he had not been defiled by contact with the theatre. For some people he would do.

Not long after the nomination of Bacon, other candidates began to appear, sponsored always by people who found Shakespeare too low-born, perhaps too earthbound, and, as they wrongly supposed, too lacking in education to have written the works which bear his name. The points of view of these sponsors are without exception snobbish or prudish, or both, and always to a degree which makes them prefer their snobbishness or prudery to information and reason. For many reasons, some of which have been mentioned earlier, the candidates found a moderate welcome, and by now the idea that perhaps Shakespeare was not Shakespeare has passed into the folklore of the western world. It might be supposed that the average person delighting in the poems and plays of Shakespeare would enjoy them with only a passing concern for their authorship (always excepting the man with a professional interest in him) and indeed this is largely the case. The Baconians of passionate conviction by whom one is cornered at dinner parties and on shipboard are in my experience persons of very pallid interest in the theatre and generally the possessors of a quite minute poetic sensibility. Almost without exception they are not historians of any species, except in as far as they have become historians to support their belief. The men who were historical scholars before they were Baconians can be counted on the fingers. I have corresponded on the matter with a professor whose subject, education, is sometimes historical, and I have read the opinions of Professor Abel Lefranc, who begins his latest book[8] by remarking that in two earlier books he had undertaken "to establish that the plays of Shakespeare were not the work of the actor from Stratford-on-Avon, but that of a member of the English aristocracy. . . ." It is the same snobbishness again, and every chapter of the occasionally illuminating book proclaims it. It should be said here that I have been using the word "Baconian" as a generic term for all persons who hold that the works of Shakespeare were written by someone else. It does not designate all of them accurately, but it is awkward to have to repeat "Baconians, Oxfordians, Derbyites, and others." My correspondent's candidate is the Earl of Oxford, Professor Lefranc's is the Earl of Derby. Professor Lefranc was a distinguished scholar before he turned Baconian, but in that he is almost alone. The ranks are peopled almost entirely by amateurs who, in as far as they enjoy distinction, have won it independently of their historical knowledge—Mark Twain, for instance. But nowadays such distinguished fellow travelers are few. Reputable intellects no longer hold Shakespeare to be either the voice of nature or a divinity, and the men of our time who can "nestle into Plato's brain" do not boggle at Shakespeare's. This may be a symptom of the irreverence of our times, but it is something more: the historical imagination is slowly learning to submit to the demands of evidence. It is a process involving some loss in the subjective splendor which certain historical studies of the last century enjoyed;

[8] Abel Lefranc, *À La Découverte de Shakespeare*, Éditions Albin Michel, Paris, Vol. I, 1945; Vol. II, 1950.

still, it cannot shackle the great spirit, and it restrains the lesser ones. We shall try to notice such of its principles as are applicable to the study of Shakespeare.

To inquire about the identity of Shakespeare the author is to ask a historical question, and the answer is to be found by a method of inquiry applicable to all questions about events which happened beyond the range of our memory. How do we know that Lincoln was assassinated or when we were born? These are matters which we all know, but *how* do we know? Well, most often we read about it, or we are told, and if our informants agree and there is no reason to suspect a conspiracy against us, we accept the information. No one is likely to question us about Lincoln's death, but there will probably be a time when we shall have to establish the date of our birth to somebody's satisfaction. The man in quest of a passport can submit a birth certificate, and if it is in order, the government is satisfied; it accepts the evidence of documents. If there is no birth certificate, a baptismal record will serve. But if there is neither, he can only consult the recollection of older friends and relatives and have them certify to it. After a little ado on the government's part, the certification will serve its practical purpose as well as the original certificates. But considered as historical evidence, is it as trustworthy? It will depend upon a number of matters.

The doctor who recorded the birth shortly after it occurred is likely to have been more accurate than the relative who made the deposition only after searching her memory—shall we assume that the relative is an aunt?—for the recollection of an event of which she knew only because she had been told. Now if the man has consulted two aunts, and if their recollections do not agree, he will have to consider an additional matter—their relative credibility. Has one a better memory than the other? Is she more truthful? Has either any reason to distort the truth? In answering these questions for himself he will be presented with a choice of probabilities, and he may have nothing better. It is clear that in so simple a matter as determining the time and place of his birth a man will have to depend upon one of a number of pieces of evidence, not all of them equally trustworthy. The least reliable will be the recollection of the relative, the most reliable the statement made by the mother's physician, a scientifically trained man who recorded the fact shortly after it occurred and sent the record to the courthouse, where it was entered on the register by a presumably competent clerk who had no incentive to falsify it.

It might happen that the record as disclosed certifies the man to have been born a little earlier than he had believed, or perhaps than he had wished. If the information is based upon the recollection of an aunt, he might persuade her that she is in error; but if he is confronted with a legal record, he will almost certainly have to defer to it. It is almost a sure thing, but not quite. Perhaps the record has been tampered with by some jealous person. So, at some expense he employs scientists to discover that the entry was made some time ago, approximately at the reported time of his birth, that it was recorded in a handwriting characteristic of the time and place in a kind of ink and on a kind of paper normally in use at the time. There have been no erasures or rewritings. The record must stand, unless, of course, it can be determined that either the doctor or the clerk was incompetent to make a simple statement or had deliberately falsified it. If, however, both are dead and there is no evidence of incompetence or villainy in their histories, it must be decided that they did their work well and that the man is as old as the record indicates. If he says that they must have falsified the record because he does not feel that old, he will persuade no one. I hope the above does not seem fanciful. Each aspect of it parallels a situation the Shakespeare scholar faces in his study of the documentary evidence of Shakespeare's career.

The following discussion refers to certain records of Shakespeare's life. They might conceivably have been made by fools, liars, or villains, but since there is not the slightest evidence for thinking so, the records must stand until they have been proved unworthy. My correspondent used to assume that Ben Jonson had been bribed to make the statements which help to establish Shakespeare's identity. The theory was very convenient, but it will not do simply to assert a thing of that sort; the statement must be proved, and there is no proof. There is not even a suggestion of proof. One may imagine, if he will, that Lincoln never really went to Ford's theatre, that on that fateful night an earlier FBI had persuaded a substitute to appear for him, that it was the impostor who was killed, and that Lincoln lived on incognito to write *The Red Badge of Courage.* Anyone to whom this fancy appeals may start a new cult with as much justification as the Baconians enjoy.

If a man is both honest and competent, he will begin a biographical study of Shakespeare by consulting the recorded facts. He will, of course, already have formed some impressions of Shakespeare, otherwise he would not want to write a biography of him; but he will hold the impressions in abeyance, for they may not be in accordance with the recorded facts. If they are not, it is the impression which will have to give way, for all sensible men will agree that what we feel about a matter must be subservient to what we come to know. If the biographer is a man of at least average sensibility, he will have many feelings about Shakespeare, based chiefly on his study of the plays and poems. Sometimes they will agree with the recorded evidence, but when they do not, he will abandon them, and in so doing he will have hit upon a principle of selection in evaluating his evidence. The principle will be that facts recorded in documents of undoubted authenticity provide the most worthy evidence he can hope to find. He will then discover that he can draw certain inferences from these facts, and that the inferences, if competently drawn, will form his next worthiest kind of evidence. Indeed, under certain circumstances some inferences will be quite indisputable. After a time he ought to be able to divide his evidence into categories and arrange them in an approximate order of their value. If he does, he will discover that he has something like the following list:

1) facts recorded in documents of undoubted authenticity
2) inferences drawn logically from these documents
3) impressions of Shakespeare formed from a reading of the plays and poems
4) legends, traditions, recorded gossip, etc.

The list will of course vary with the biographical problems. Let us consider what some of the evidence in the first category will tell us about Shakespeare. We shall not consider all the facts in the category, for they are to be found in countless books, and we do not want to be more tedious than need be. The baptism of William, son of John Shakespeare, was recorded in the Baptismal Register of Stratford-on-Avon on 26 April 1564. There is no record of his birth, but we need not be surprised. Even today the compulsory registration of births is far from universal, and in most civilized communities it is a fairly recent custom. In Pennsylvania, for instance, such registration was not required until 1906. Presumably Shakespeare, in accordance with the custom of his time, was baptized a few days after his birth. The entry in the Baptismal Register establishes the date of his baptism and his parentage. The license for his marriage is recorded in the Episcopal Register of the Diocese of Worcester under the date of 27 November 1582. The marriage bond, permitting the marriage with one asking of the bans, was entered in the same register on the following day. Almost exactly six months later, 26 May 1583, the baptism of his first child, Susanna, was recorded. Less than two years later, 2 February 1584 (1585 according to the modern calendar) the same register recorded the baptism of his twins, Hamnet and Judith. He made his will on 26 March 1616 and was buried in the Church of the Holy Trinity, Stratford, 25 April 1616. The burial is recorded in the Stratford Burial Register. These are some of the facts which cannot be denied. They could be discredited only by establishing that the records are not authentic, but the records have been subjected to scrutiny, and they must stand.

He is first referred to as a man of the London theatre in 1592. We do not know when he went to London. Presumably he had been in Stratford when the twins were born; certainly he was there when they were begot; but of his career after the begetting of the twins and before the reference of 1592 there is no clear evidence. However, there can be no doubt that the William Shakespeare of the Stratford records and the William Shakespeare of the London theatre are the same man. Contemporary comment of undoubted authenticity establishes the identity of the man from Stratford and the London playwright and actor, and all relevant documentary evidence supports the identification. It would be both tedious and unnecessary to repeat the evidence here. All reputable biographies of Shakespeare, and all Shakespearean handbooks, present the evidence, and every library in all English-speaking countries is rich in them. The evidence is available to everyone who wishes to see. Moreover, there is no contemporary evidence to the contrary. In short, we know who wrote Shakespeare's plays on precisely the same sort of evidence as that which tells us how Marie Antoinette met her death or who was the first president of the United States. We know it because it is recorded in documents of undoubted authenticity and because there is no documentary evidence suggesting anything to the contrary.

If we cannot accept this evidence, we cannot accept the evidence of other documents, and there is no history beyond the memory of living man. It is as simple and as clear as that. Shakespeare's authorship stands, or all recorded history beyond the memory of living man disappears with it.

Thus far our historian has dealt with incontestable records, but he wants to know more. What inferences can he draw from the records about, say, Shakespeare's education? It follows from the fact of Shakespeare's having written the plays that he was a highly literate person and that he had been educated somewhere. Presumably he went to school. Where? Well, there was a free grammar school in Stratford during Shakespeare's youth; it is still there, and still functioning. It was a good school, and it existed for just such boys as the sons of John Shakespeare. Unfortunately for us, the school at that time did not preserve a record of the boys attending it, and there is no way of knowing which of the Stratford boys studied there and which did not. As for Shakespeare, it is more reasonable to suppose that he went to school than that he was educated by private tutors, and it is more reasonable to suppose that he went to school in Stratford than in another town. The probability is great enough to make a discussion of it sound a bit silly. Still, we do not know the place of his education with the certainty with which we know the date of his baptism. We *know* some facts of his career; our conclusion about the place of his schooling rests on a balance of probabilities. If a document were to be discovered establishing that he went to school elsewhere, the belief that he went to school in Stratford would have to give way to it.

When a Baconian assumes the inadequacy of Shakespeare's education and his inability to have produced the plays which he says are attributed to him, he is begging a question and denying a fact. The record *is* that this man, William Shakespeare, of Stratford-on-Avon, wrote the plays. That is the fact the Baconian denies. And since he wrote them, it follows that he was competent to write them; and that is the question which the Baconian begs. When the biographer considers *if* Shakespeare was educated, or that he was not, he is ignoring fact in favor of presumption. The fact remains a fact, and the more the presumption is speciously documented—for there can be no true documentation of it—the more presumptuous it becomes.

The reader who would like to see an honest Baconian at work is referred to *Will Shakespeare and the Dyer's Hand*, by Alden Brooks, which concludes that the plays were written by Sir Edward Dyer. There can be no doubt of its sincerity, and the labor that went into it is apparent on each of its seven hundred pages. It was handsomely published by Charles Scribner's Sons in 1943, presumably because some members of the Scribner staff were persuaded of its worth. Brooks simply assumes that the man who wrote the plays 1) must have been a courtier, 2) must have been well over forty at the time the sonnets were written, 3) must have suffered from ill health and "at the end may have suffered a nervous breakdown," 4) must have died in the winter of 1608, and some fifty other matters. These criteria, reasonably enough, Shakespeare does not meet, and, surprisingly enough, Sir Edward Dyer does. But how the author came by these criteria seven hundred closely packed pages and an earlier book cannot make clear. They are in part formulated from impressions arising from the study of Shakespeare's works, but by what wayward processes only heaven knows.

The impressions one forms of Shakespeare from reading his works are not necessarily fanciful. Every reader will know that Shakespeare was a man who wrote well, could tell a story with the best, had unusual powers of observation, wide sympathies, a capacity for great emotion, exceptional understanding of his fellow men, and so on; but without other sources of information he will not know how Shakespeare acquired these capacities or to what they led him on a given day. He will not assume that the dramatist had literally experienced everything he wrote about; after all, he wrote much on suicide. Nor will he suppose that what a poet says of himself in a poem is literally true. When Shakespeare says in the sonnets that he is old, he does not mean that he is decrepit. He means that he is old in comparison with the young man and the young woman, that, in short, he *feels* old. When he says that he is lame (what he really says is, "Speak of my lameness and I straight will halt") he does not mean that he limps or is willing to limp on demand. There is such a thing as metaphor. On the other hand, the poet is not always speaking metaphorically, and he *might* mean that he limps. There seems to be a choice of interpretations. How free is it? The external evidence does not mention the matter, but it does say that Shakespeare was an actor. Since actors are not normally lame, the probability on documented evidence is that he did not limp, and the idea that he did, which had somewhat less than an even chance of truth in the first place, must give way to the stronger probability that he did not. When the nearest we can get to truth on the evidence at hand is a balance of probabilities, we must as honest men prefer the greater until a still greater probability or the plain truth is established. This business of the lameness is a silly matter. One is surprised that so many commentators have been worried by it and have, in turn, worried it themselves.

There is a larger matter more deserving of attention, and it, too, rests on an impression from the sonnets. It is the allegation of homosexuality which has been made from time to time and continues to be made in various publications. In the most notable instances the charge has been made by men of known homosexual experience, who, like members of all minority groups, are anxious to increase their numbers.

But they are not alone, and, in any case, the seriousness of an allegation does not depend upon the personality of the man making it. By now the idea has been stated often enough to have a marginal place in the Shakespeare folklore. A writer in *The Partisan Review*[9] refers in passing to "the Shakespearean myth of good homosexual love opposed to an evil heterosexual attachment," and from time to time one encounters such things as the manly compassion Wyndham Lewis feels for Shakespeare: "To have his 'normal' woman-love castrated, and to be turned into a female at an early age, must have a considerable effect upon the mentality of a man. Or to be born sexually agressive but so constituted that the usual female dish provided by nature is turned away from with disgust, must also leave its little mark on the mind."[10] The notion of Shakespeare's homosexuality is current, and it is not diminished by either the silence of Shakespeare's more temperate critics or the indignant denials of the more muscular commentators who rise up every now and then and vigorously thrust the matter away. It will be well to look at the basis of the charge.

Although in all of Shakespeare's works no subjects are accorded more importance than love and sex, very little is said of homosexuality. In no instance is it a dominant motive in the behavior of a character. Lesbianism is neither mentioned nor suggested, and homosexuality between men is seldom referred to, the strongest reference being Thersites' remark that Patroclus is thought to be Achilles' "masculine whore." There is nothing in any of the plays to suggest that Shakespeare thought the idea of homosexuality of any importance in the interpretation of character. When the notion of homosexuality in Shakespeare occurs to disinterested persons, it arises from the attitude expressed toward the young

[9] June 1948, p. 668.

[10] Wyndham Lewis, *The Lion and the Fox*, Harper and Brothers, New York and London, n.d., p. 153.

man of the sonnets, and more particularly from the terms by which he is addressed. He is sometimes called "friend," but the commoner terms are "love" and "my love." These are not the terms in which a man of our time addresses a friend, and it is quite natural that they should suggest abnormality to readers not widely familiar with the literature of the Renaissance, who in this post-Freudian era see clues which their predecessors passed by. It must be remembered that the meanings of words shift with the years, and that while it may be true that basic emotions do not change, it is quite true that the concepts in which emotions are expressed change very radically, that a term which seemed inevitably apt to the man of one century may seem forced and distorted to a later time.

To Shakespeare and his contemporaries the words "love" and "lover" as used between men did mean "friendship" and "friend," and were so used throughout Shakespeare's works. "I tell thee, fellow, thy general is my lover," said Menenius of Coriolanus; and when Brutus addresses the crowd as "Romans, countrymen, lovers," he means by "lovers" precisely what Mr. Roosevelt in his radio addresses meant by "my friends." This was the usage of the day. There was also the Renaissance concept of the superiority of the friendship of man to man over the affection of man for woman. One gathers that the Renaissance expression of this notion was a kind of tribute to the neo-Platonic tradition, spoken in all sincerity, much as an American in full allegiance to his democratic heritage speaks of the equal rights of all citizens, but without, it would appear, always being prepared to express his allegiance in action. And doubtless there were times when the preference for male friendship over an erotic attachment represented the attitude of a given man toward a particular situation, as in the circumstances revealed by the later sonnets. But at the moment we are concerned with the general situation. The superiority of friendship was part of the belief of the age, and people heard it with no sense of strangeness. That is the important and relevant thing. When the warrior Aufidius welcomes Coriolanus to the ranks of the Volsces, he says,

> Know thou first,
> I lov'd the maid I married; never man
> Sighed truer breath; but that I see thee here,
> Thou noble thing, more dances my rapt heart
> Than when I first my wedded mistress saw
> Bestride my threshold.[11]

The idea here serves to express the welcome in the strongest possible terms. Comparable uses of the idea are found in other plays, but it seemed best to refer to *Coriolanus*, for never were characters more extroverted, more completely and incontrovertibly masculine than Coriolanus and his associates.

It might be argued that there are many meanings of "love," that although Shakespeare used the word to mean "friendship," he also used it to mean sexual attraction, and that it is so used in the sonnets. One might argue the possibility of someday discovering a document establishing the homosexuality which the sonnets suggest to some readers. May I state that although such an eventuality would surprise me, I should not be deeply chagrined. Many men of irregular lives have left a great legacy to the world, and the wise man will cherish his inheritance while thinking little on the weaknesses of the departed great. It is a small man who cannot overlook a sin of the flesh on the part of another who has been dead for over three centuries. It would be idle to urge this view on those who for their own good reasons resist it. I state my attitude in passing because it seems to me that a reader is entitled to know the point of view from which a writer speaks. If it is urged that even though what has

[11] *Coriolanus*, 4.5.119-124.

been said earlier is true, the attraction might still be a homosexual one, it could only be answered that it might. But we should ask what the probability is.

The impression which sometimes arises from the sonnets is not the only possible interpretation of them; it is clearly not the most informed one, but it indicates a possibility. What other possibilities are there? and what is the evidence on which they rest? The only incontrovertible evidence about Shakespeare's sexual life is this: at the age of eighteen he married a woman eight years his senior. Six months after the marriage he was a father. One year and nine months later he was again a father, this time of twins. It is clear that at an early age he was actively heterosexual. There is no external evidence suggesting that he was homosexual, and of course there is no statement that he was not. If a man does not beat his wife, his forbearance is not recorded. There can be no absolute proof one way or the other. We must be content with probabilities, and the balance of probability is that a man who was actively heterosexual in his youth did not later become deeply involved in a homosexual episode. It has, of course, happened, but statistically speaking, it is more likely not to happen. The probability is that it did not happen to Shakespeare.

However, this matter cannot be covered adequately in an *either / or* discussion. If we have learned anything from modern psychology, we should have lost faith in the old rigid distinction between normal and abnormal. The world is not divided into sheep and goats, at least not yet. "Males," in Mr. Kinsey's words, "do not represent two discrete populations, heterosexual and homosexual. . . . It is a fundamental of taxonomy that nature rarely deals in discrete categories. Only the human mind invents categories and tries to force facts into separate pigeon-holes. The living world is a continuum in each and every one of its aspects."[12] We may take it that no one in past ages was more aware of this than Shakespeare. There is no great writer with whom the disregard of categories is so striking; and it grew with his maturing. He adapted, almost to the point of obliteration, the *genres* with which he worked, and he is, par excellence, the master of the in-between-places of the soul. It cannot be supposed for a moment that he was unaware of sexual ambivalence, or that he avoided it in his plays for reasons of propriety. It must be supposed that he avoided it because it did not seem to him to be a significant factor in the life he knew.

Probably no one, not even Wilde, imagined him to have been the sort of homosexual whose physique and manner proclaims his nature; and surely no one, even though he had no source of information other than the sonnets, would think him to have been exclusively homosexual. If the matter is to be thought of at all, it must be asked whether the sonnets reflect a homosexual episode in an otherwise heterosexual life. What on a priori grounds is the probability of this? Statistical studies of erotic behavior have been reserved for our own times, and while the relevance of our own mores to the culture of another time and place may be questioned, there is not much other evidence by which the matter may be sensibly considered. The study made by Mr. Kinsey and his associates finds that only "fifty percent of the population is exclusively heterosexual throughout its adult life," and that only four percent is exclusively homosexual. It follows that "nearly half of the population engages in heterosexual and homosexual activities, or reacts to persons of both sexes in the course of their adult lives."[13] Thus statistical probability suggests that there is a little less than an even chance of a man's having a homosexual episode in his life, and even

[12] A. C. Kinsey and associates, *Sexual Behavior in the Human Male*, W. B. Saunders Company, Philadelphia and London, 1948, p. 639.
[13] *Ibid.*, p. 565.

here there is the nature of the episode to be considered, for not all of the forty-six percent express their impulses in action. What Mr. Kinsey means by "engages in" is clear enough. By "reacts to" he means the awareness of an impulse which for one reason or another is denied. He tells us elsewhere in his study that thirty-seven percent of the men interviewed had engaged in homosexuality at one time or another. The percentage of those who simply "react" is apparently nine. Therefore the abstract chance of a man's engaging in such activity is roughly one in three, and the chances of his "reacting" to another man is one in eleven.

There is still another possibility, one obviously beyond the range of a study based on interviews. It can be best indicated by Michel, the hero of Gide's *L'Immoraliste*, a man who never committed a homosexual act, who never understood, who was never, in fact, fully aware of the impulses stirring within him. It would require either a full case history or omniscience to assign Shakespeare to this category, and we can pretend to the possession of neither. He does not appear to have engaged in homosexual activity, and in general his reactions are the essence of his plays. They do not even suggest a homosexual interest. He tells in one of his sonnets that he was aware of a certain femininity in the young man. It is, he suggests, almost as though he were in love with him; but he laughingly denies any erotic interest. It is possible to construe this as a sexual interest of which he was not aware, or to which he would not admit, but on the evidence at hand that is the way of madness. To follow this idea further would land us in the position of a dinner partner I once had while on a busman's holiday at one of my favorite places, The University of Rochester, where the college for men and the college for women are, as Mr. Kinsey would say, discrete. In speaking of a professor, a recent widower, who preferred teaching in the college for women, my partner remarked, "It is, of course, compensation." And of another

professor who preferred teaching in the college for men:
"Clearly suppressed homosexuality." In this country all roads
lead to Vienna. Let us move elsewhere.

The honest truth is that all reasonable considerations suggest the probability that Shakespeare was not homosexual.
The claim for heterosexuality rests on probability and irrefu-
table external evidence; that for homosexuality on a problem-
atic interpretation of the uncertain biographical value of
poetic composition. There is some further confirmation of
this conclusion. The best of the sonnets to the young man
are deeply moving poems. If we assume them to express a
personal emotion, we must assume that the emotion went
deep. If we further assume an abnormal attachment, it will
follow that the attachment was not a casual one. If it was
abnormal, it was deeply abnormal, and we would expect it
to appear in his other works. This it never does. If on the
other hand we turn to the sonnets with the homosexual interpretation consistently in mind, we shall find that it defeats
itself. The young man is not the only male person referred
to in terms of love. Dead friends of Shakespeare are mentioned as "my lovers gone."[14] The young man is told that
if the poems endure he will live "in lovers' eyes."[15] In this
view the homosexuality extends itself to times before and
after the years in which the sonnets were composed; and it
will appear that the other poets writing verses to the young
man were sexually attached to him, and were known to be.
Consistently applied, the interpretation discloses a morass of
homosexuality incredible in its proportions.

There is one other matter. It is known that the sonnets
circulated in manuscript among Shakespeare's friends, and
widely enough for a copy to find a piratical printing. It is
one thing to have a homosexual devotion to another man,
and it is quite another to advertise it. Life in Elizabeth's
time was more free than in our own, though not as free as

---

[14] Sonnet 31.   [15] Sonnet 55.

is often supposed. But whatever the freedom, it did not extend to an acceptance of homosexuality. If Shakespeare had proclaimed such a passion, it is likely that it would have been commented on, and it is possible that some of the comment would have survived. The absence of such comment is negative evidence and far from conclusive, yet it should be remembered that negative evidence is all one may hope for in regard to a nonexistent matter. If we were to invent a like charge against, say, Sir Thomas Browne, basing it on his eulogy of friendship and his relative undervaluing of erotic love, honest men could only reply by calling our attention to Browne's ten children and the absence of evidence to the contrary. With two exceptions the contemporary references to Shakespeare are laudatory. On his death bed Robert Greene spoke in professional envy of him, and when he was in his cups Sir William Davenant liked to imply that Shakespeare was more than his godfather. He would rather have been a poet's bastard than an innkeeper's heir. Even John Aubrey, whose eye for scandal is legendary, found no charge against him. It was Aubrey who wrote of Ben Jonson that he "had one eye lower than t'other and bigger, like Clun the player." Then of his own generosity he added, "Perhaps he begot Clun." Aubrey said of Shakespeare that he worked hard and "would not be debauched." Recent studies have hunted for Shakespeare the man in his use of imagery, and have had extraordinarily little to say about his attitudes toward sex. But in the introduction to his recent glossary of Shakespeare's sexual terms Eric Partridge[16] finds that the point of view disclosed by the rich use of erotic language is altogether masculine.

The fourth kind of evidence, tradition and legend, is the least reliable of all. "This account," writes Aubrey, after one of his most fantastic and libelous anecdotes, "I had from

[16] Eric Partridge, *Shakespeare's Bawdy*, E. P. Dutton & Co., New York; 1948.

my honoured friend Old Mistress Tyndale, whose grand-
father, Sir William Stafford, was an intimate acquaintance
of this Sir —— Roper, who told him the story."[17] (The
preceding blank is Aubrey's. The name he searched for and
could not find was William.) It is the sort of pedigree most
legends have, although the pedigree is not often set forth
with such a wealth of self-revealing worthlessness. Yet legends exist, and the biographer is free to use them provided
he does not pretend that they are anything more than they
are. The story that Shakespeare as a young man poached
deer in the park of Sir Thomas Lucy did not die when it
became known that Sir Thomas did not have a park. A legend
does not live on its details, and common people know this
very well. They do not care whether the scene of the alleged
poaching was or was not a park, or to whom it belonged.
The essence of the story is that Shakespeare was a young
man of high spirits, and this is probable enough. A biographer
does not need to use the legend, but if he is a man of good
sense he will not trouble to refute it; and if he is a biographer
of any distinction he will not build upon it. A legend will
do no harm if it is used to underline what is known on
other grounds. Thomas Fuller was eight years old when
Shakespeare died, and he cannot have been a party to his
table talk. What he says of it may be his invention, but
if it is, it is spun out of likely material: "Many were the
wit-combats betwixt him and Ben Jonson, which two I behold like a Spanish great galleon and an English man-of-
war; Master Jonson (like the former) was built far higher
in learning, solid, but slow in his performances; Shakespeare
with the English man-of-war, lesser in bulk, but lighter in
sailing, could turn with all tides, tack about, and take ad-
vantage of all winds by the quickness of his wit and invention." We can depend upon it that if Fuller had reversed

[17] John Aubrey, *Brief Lives*, the "notes" on Sir Thomas More.

the roles of Jonson and Shakespeare, his paragraph would never have found even partial credence.

In legend there is a kind of negative testimony in the direction of truth. Some things are not said of certain people. Not everything said of Nero can be believed, but no one has ever dared say that he was nice to his mother. In March of 1602 a Mr. Curle told John Manningham something that people were saying about Shakespeare: "Upon a time when Burbage played Richard Third there was a citizen grew so far in liking with him that before she went from the play she appointed him to come that night unto her by the name of Richard the Third. Shakespeare overhearing their conclusion, went before, was entertained, and at his game ere Burbage came. Then message being brought that Richard the Third was at the door, Shakespeare caused return to be made that William the Conqueror was before Richard the Third. Shakespeare's name was William." This is an old story, older than Shakespeare, and found with other names in other lands. Like many basic plots it survives in tradition, and from time to time is no doubt renewed by experience. Although it probably did not happen to Shakespeare, it was found credible in 1602; and it may be that it is. The credence we give or withhold will depend upon the sort of person we are and what impressions of Shakespeare we have consciously or unconsciously gained from his works.

Index

DRAMABOOKS